spiralize
every day

**80 RECIPES TO HELP
REPLACE YOUR CARBS**

DENISE SMART

hamlyn

An Hachette UK Company
www.hachette.co.uk

First published in Great Britain in 2016 by Hamlyn,
a division of
Octopus Publishing Group Ltd
Carmelite House
50 Victoria Embankment
London EC4Y 0DZ
www.octopusbooks.co.uk

ISBN 978-0-600-63448-5

A CIP catalogue record for this book is available from
the British Library.

Printed and bound in China

10 9 8 7 6 5 4 3 2 1

Standard level spoon measurements are used in
all recipes.
1 tablespoon = one 15 ml spoon
1 teaspoon = one 5 ml spoon

Both imperial and metric measurements have been
given in all recipes. Use one set of measurements
only and not a mixture of both.

Eggs should be medium unless otherwise stated.
The Department of Health advises that eggs should
not be consumed raw.

Always check the labels of preprepared ingredients
to make sure they do not contain ingredients that
are not suitable if you are following a vegetarian,
vegan, gluten-free or low-carb diet. For vegetarian
recipes, check cheese labels to ensure they are
suitable for vegetarians and use vegetarian pasta
cheese instead of traditional Parmesan, which is
made with animal rennet.

contents

introduction

A spiralizer is an affordable, easy-to-use cutting machine with a selection of blades that you can use to create a variety of noodles and ribbons from vegetables and fruit. It can help you to save time as it's really quick and easy to prepare fruit and vegetables using a spiralizer. And spiralizing can also reduce cooking times because many of the vegetables and fruit prepared in this way can be eaten raw or just cooked very lightly, which also means that all nutrients are retained.

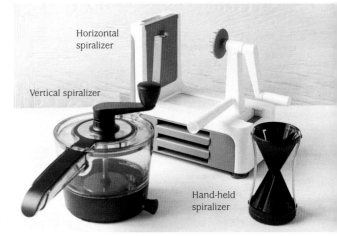

Horizontal spiralizer

Vertical spiralizer

Hand-held spiralizer

spiralizing and a healthy diet

A spiralizer is the ideal gadget for health-conscious cooks as it can help you to cut back on refined carbohydrates, such as pasta and rice, by replacing them with spiralized fruit and vegetables so that you can enjoy your meals while eating fewer calories.

Carbohydrates make up an essential part of our diet and are needed for our main energy supply; they are available in three forms, sugar, starch and dietary fibre. Some foods are high in carbohydrates, such as pasta, bread and many processed foods, but by eating them in an unprocessed form, such as fruit and vegetables,

you can absorb the best nutrients from them and eat fewer calories. A 75 g (3 oz) portion of cooked spaghetti contains about 270 calories and 55 g (2 oz) of carbohydrate compared to about 50 calories and 10 g (½ oz) of carbohydrate for a bowl of courgetti made from 1 large courgette.

A spiralizer will also encourage you to include more fruit and vegetables in your diet and can be a life-saver for those following special diets, such as low carb, gluten free, paleo and raw food. Always check the labels of preprepared ingredients if you are following a gluten-free diet to make sure they do not contain any wheat, either as an ingredient (for example, soy sauce) or through cross-contamination (for example, oats). Gluten-free versions are often available and may be used instead.

Cheese is a good source of protein if you are a vegetarian, but always check the label to ensure that it is suitable for vegetarians and doesn't contain animal rennet. Some hard cheeses, such as Parmesan, and other traditional cheeses, such as Gorgonzola and buffalo mozzarella, are still made with animal rennet, although increasingly cheese is being made with 'microbial enzymes' or 'vegetable rennet', both of which are suitable

Each recipe in this book includes quick-reference symbols so that you can see at a glance whether a recipe is low carb, gluten free, vegetarian or vegan.

(gf) gluten free

(lc) low carb

(v) vegetarian

(vg) vegan

for vegetarians. Vegetarian pasta cheese is a great alternative to Parmesan cheese, and cheeses such as goats' cheese, feta, ricotta and mozzarella are also suitable.

choosing a spiralizer

There are many brands on the market, but all essentially work in the same way. The larger horizontal and vertical ones are better for heavier root vegetables and everyday use, but small hand-held ones are ideal if you are cooking for one or for occasional use or for creating garnishes.

Spiralizers usually come with several different blades, each of which creates a different shape. For this book, I used a horizontal spiralizer with three blades, which I have called the 3 mm (⅛ inch) spaghetti blade, the 6 mm (¼ inch) flat noodle blade and the ribbon blade.

6 mm (¼ inch) flat noodle blade

Ribbon blade

3 mm (⅛ inch) spaghetti blade

how to use a horizontal spiralizer

1 Attach the machine to the worktop using the suction feet or lever.

2 Insert the blade you wish to use into the machine.

3 Prepare the fruit or vegetable according to the recipe: peel it, if required, trim off the ends to make a flat surface and cut in half widthways, if necessary.

4 Attach one end of the prepared fruit or vegetable to the blade and then clamp the other end of the vegetable to the spiky grip on the crank handle.

5 Grasp the side handle for leverage, turn the crank handle and apply a little pressure so that the fruit or vegetable is pressed

between the blade and the handle – this will create spirals or ribbons.

6 Finally, remove the long core and a round disc that remains at the end of the spiralizing process (this can be chopped up and used to make soups, if you like).

how to make vegetable rices

1 Spiralize your chosen vegetable, using the spaghetti or noodle blade. Cauliflower should just be broken into florets.

2 Place the spiralized vegetable or cauliflower florets in a food processor and pulse until the mixture resembles rice.

tips for successful spiralizing

• Choose firm fruit and vegetables without stones, seeds or hollow centres: the only exceptions are butternut squash (just use the non-bulbous end) and green papaya.

• Vegetables and fruit should not be soft or juicy – pineapples, melons and aubergines will fall apart when you spiralize them.

• Choose vegetables that are as straight as possible. Occasionally you may have to re-centre the vegetables to avoid half-moon shapes.

• Make sure the ends of fruit and vegetables are as flat as possible by slicing a small piece off either end. Uneven ends can make it difficult to secure the fruit or vegetable to the spiralizer and may cause them to dislodge or misalign.

• If you find that a fruit or vegetable is not spiralizing very well, it may be because there is not a large enough surface area for the spiralizer to grip to. For best results, lengths should be no longer than 12 cm (5 inches) and about 3.5 cm (1½ inches) in diameter. Cut any large vegetables in half widthways.

• You will be left with a long core and a round disc at the end of the spiralizing process. Save these cores to use when making soups or for snacks.

• A lot of juice is squeezed out of fruit and vegetables when you spiralize them, especially from courgettes, carrots, cucumber, potatoes, apples and pears. Just pat the spirals dry on kitchen paper before use.

• Be careful when cleaning your spiralizer as the blades are very sharp. Wash the machine in hot, soapy water and use a small kitchen brush or toothbrush to clean the blades.

cooking tips

• Spiralized vegetables can be eaten raw or cooked very quickly. The best cooking methods are stir-frying, steaming or adding to sauces and stocks. You can also bake and roast spiralized vegetables such as potatoes, parsnips, beetroot and butternut squash in half the time you would cook large chunks of the same vegetables.

• Some vegetable rices, such as beetroot, carrot, courgette and daikon radish, can be used raw. Alternatively, lightly sauté in a little oil or simmer in a little stock or sauce. They will take a very short time to cook.

• It is very easy to overcook vegetable spaghetti, so keep a close eye on it while cooking to make sure it doesn't fall apart.

• As a general rule, the harder the vegetable, the longer the cooking time.

• Make sauces thicker than you usually would as certain vegetable noodles, especially courgettes, will release extra juice into your sauce.

• Pat vegetables dry on kitchen paper, especially courgettes and cucumber.

• Cook your spaghetti or noodles separately, before stirring into your sauce.

storing tips

Most spiralized vegetables and vegetable rices can be stored in an airtight container in the refrigerator for up to 4 days. The exceptions are spiralized cucumber, which will only keep for about 2 days because of its high water content, and apples, pears and potatoes, which quickly oxidize and turn brown and so are best prepared as needed.

which fruit and vegetables can I use?

Apples There's no need to peel or core apples, just trim the ends and spiralize whole. Remember that the spiralized apple will turn brown very quickly so use immediately or dress with lemon juice.

Beetroot There's no need to peel beetroot, just wash the skin, flatten the ends and spiralize whole.

Broccoli Don't throw away broccoli stems when you cook broccoli – the stems spiralize really well.

Butternut squash To avoid the seeds, you should only use the non-bulbous end of the squash. Snip any really long strands of spiralized squash into smaller pieces using scissors.

Carrots Choose large carrots for spiralizing.

Celeriac The best way to prepare this root vegetable is to use a sharp knife to remove the knobbly bits from the celeriac and then peel it, cut it in half widthways and trim to make the ends flat.

Courgettes Forget about cooking with regular pasta, spiralized courgettes make perfect courgetti (courgette spaghetti).

Cucumbers Once you've spiralized the cucumber you just need to pat the spirals or ribbons dry.

Daikon radish (mooli) Spiralized daikon radish makes a great alternative to rice noodles.

Green papaya You can find green papaya in Asian supermarkets. Although it is hollow it attaches to the spiralizer well.

Green plantains Choose plantains that are as straight as possible and remove the tough outer green skin.

Jerusalem artichokes Choose large artichokes. There's no need to peel these knobbly vegetables, all you need to do is wash them. If you're not using the spiralized artichokes immediately, place them in a bowl of water with a little lemon juice to prevent them discolouring.

Kohlrabi Choose small kohlrabi about the size of a large apple. Prepare by peeling the outside and trimming the ends.

Onions Onions can be spiralized whole – all you need to do is trim the ends before you start.

Parsnips Choose large, fat parsnips for best results when spiralizing.

Pears Choose firm pears for spiralizing as pears that are too ripe will add too much moisture to some of the dessert recipes. To prepare the pears for spiralizing, just trim down the pointy ends.

Potatoes and sweet potatoes Prepare potatoes by either scrubbing or peeling and then trim the ends and cut in half widthways if very large. Sweet potatoes are great for adding colour to a dish.

Swedes Peel off the outside skin and cut the swede into large chunks with flat ends to attach to the spiralizer.

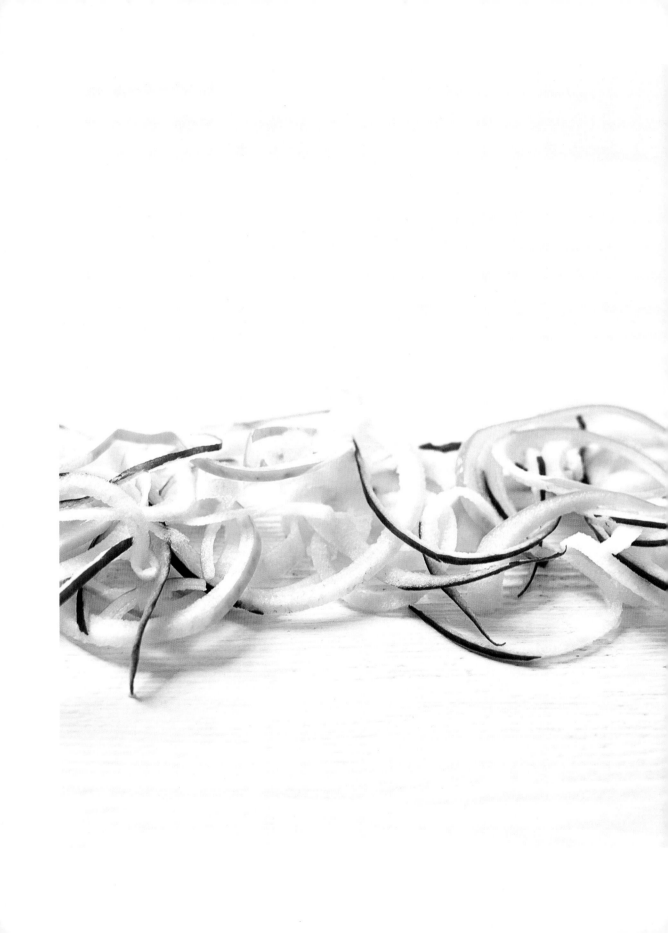

breakfasts and brunch

apple and blueberry buckwheat pancakes with maple syrup

Serves 4
Prepare in 10 minutes
Cook in 12–15 minutes

2 red eating apples, ends trimmed

150 g (5 oz) buckwheat flour

½ teaspoon salt

2 teaspoons gluten-free baking powder

2 tablespoons caster sugar

300 ml (½ pint) buttermilk

1 egg

125 g (4 oz) fresh blueberries

1 tablespoon sunflower oil

To serve
handful of blueberries

maple syrup or honey

Using a spiralizer fitted with a 3 mm (⅛ inch) spaghetti blade, spiralize the apple.

Sift the flour, salt and baking powder into a large bowl and stir in the sugar. Whisk together the buttermilk and egg in a jug. Gradually beat the buttermilk mixture into the flour to make a smooth batter. Stir in the spiralized apple and the blueberries.

Heat a large nonstick frying pan over a medium heat. Dip a scrunched up piece of kitchen paper into the oil and carefully use this to grease the hot pan. Drop 4 large tablespoons of the batter into the pan (this will make 4 small pancakes) and cook for 2–3 minutes until bubbles start to appear on the surface and the underside is golden brown. Flip over the pancakes and cook for a further 2 minutes. Keep the pancakes warm while you cook the remaining batter, greasing the pan with a little more oil if necessary.

Place 3 pancakes on each plate, add some blueberries and a drizzle of maple syrup or honey and serve immediately.

Make these tasty breakfast bars in advance so you always have an energy-boosting snack in your storecupboard.

carrot and banana breakfast bars

Makes 16
Prepare in 10 minutes
Cook in 35 minutes

3 tablespoons coconut or olive oil, plus extra for greasing

3 tablespoons date nectar or honey

4 tablespoons crunchy peanut butter

2 carrots, about 250 g (8 oz), peeled, ends trimmed and halved widthways

3 overripe bananas

200 g (7 oz) raisins or sultanas

300 g (10 oz) gluten-free rolled oats

Grease a 28 x 18 cm (11 x 7 inch) baking tin with a little oil.

Place the date nectar or honey, peanut butter and oil in a small saucepan and cook over a low heat, stirring from time to time, until melted.

Meanwhile, using a spiralizer fitted with a 3 mm (⅛ inch) spaghetti blade, spiralize the carrots. Roughly snip any really long spirals in half with scissors.

Place the bananas in a large bowl and mash them with a fork, then stir in the spiralized carrots, raisins or sultanas and oats. Pour over the peanut butter mixture and mix well until all the ingredients are combined.

Spoon the mixture into the prepared tin and flatten the top with the back of a spoon. Bake in a preheated oven, 180°C (350°F), Gas Mark 4, for 30 minutes, until golden brown. Remove from the oven and leave to cool in the tin for 10–15 minutes. Mark into 16 bars and leave to cool completely in the tin. The breakfast bars can be stored for up to 2 days in an airtight container.

These crunchy bars require very little cooking – all you need to do is toast the oats and quinoa.

peanut butter, quinoa and apple bars

Makes 8

Prepare in 5 minutes, plus chilling

Cook in 10 minutes

150 g (5 oz) gluten-free rolled oats

125 g (4 oz) uncooked quinoa

1 tablespoon chia seeds or linseeds

2 red eating apples, ends trimmed

125 g (4 oz) crunchy peanut butter

½ teaspoon sea salt

75 g (3 oz) honey

2 tablespoons apple juice

1 tablespoon coconut oil

Line a 20 cm (8 inch) square tin with nonstick baking paper.

Spread out the oats and quinoa on a large nonstick baking sheet and bake in a preheated oven, 180°C (350°F), Gas Mark 4, for 10 minutes, stirring once, until lightly toasted. Tip into a bowl and stir in the seeds.

Meanwhile, using a spiralizer fitted with a 6 mm (¼ inch) flat noodle blade, spiralize the apples.

Place the peanut butter, sea salt, honey, apple juice and coconut oil in a saucepan and cook over a low heat, stirring until the mixture is smooth and creamy. Stir in the spiralized apples and leave to cool for a few minutes.

Stir the peanut mixture into the oat mixture and mix until well combined. Spoon the mixture into the prepared tin and spread out evenly. Chill in the refrigerator for about 1 hour or until the mixture has hardened and set.

Remove from the tin and cut into 8 bars. The bars can be stored for up to 3–4 days in an airtight container in the refrigerator.

This buttery French toast is topped with caramelized pears. If you prefer, you could replace the pears with apples.

cinnamon and pear brioche French toast

Using a spiralizer fitted with a ribbon blade, spiralize the pear.

Melt the butter and sugar in a large frying pan, add the spiralized pear and cook over a medium heat for 5–6 minutes, stirring occasionally, until lightly caramelized. Set aside.

In a shallow dish, whisk together the egg, cinnamon and sugar, then whisk in the milk. Add the slices of bread, leave to soak in the mixture for a few minutes and then turn over and leave to stand until all the egg mixture is absorbed.

Melt a little butter in a frying pan over a medium heat. Add the bread and cook for 2–3 minutes on each side, until golden. Serve immediately, topped with the caramelized pear.

Serves 2
Prepare in 5 minutes
Cook in 10–15 minutes

1 large pear, pointy end trimmed

15 g (½ oz) butter, plus extra for frying

2 teaspoons soft brown sugar

For the toast

1 large egg

½ teaspoon ground cinnamon

1 tablespoon caster sugar

50 ml (2 fl oz) milk

2 thick slices brioche bread

This classic breakfast cereal is also delicious as a crunchy snack. It can be stored for up to 2 days in an airtight container.

honey-roasted apple granola

Serves 4

Prepare in 10 minutes, plus cooling

Cook in 35–40 minutes

5 tablespoons honey

2 tablespoons coconut or olive oil

2 red eating apples, ends trimmed

125 g (4 oz) gluten-free rolled oats

125 g (4 oz) uncooked white quinoa

100 g (3½ oz) whole skin-on almonds, roughly chopped

50 g (2 oz) sunflower seeds

50 g (2 oz) sesame seeds

To serve

milk or yogurt

fresh fruit

Warm the honey and oil in a small saucepan over a low heat.

Meanwhile, using a spiralizer fitted with a ribbon blade, spiralize the apples.

Place the oats, quinoa, almonds and seeds in a large bowl, add the spiralized apples and mix well. Pour over the warm honey mixture and stir well to combine.

Spread out the mixture on a large nonstick baking sheet and bake in a preheated oven, 150°C (300°F), Gas Mark 2, for 30–35 minutes, until golden, stirring once. Remove from the oven and leave to cool and harden.

Serve with milk or yogurt and fresh fruit.

Mix up the ingredients the night before and you will have a delicious breakfast ready in the morning.

autumn bircher muesli with almond milk

 (gf) (v) (vg)

Serves 2

Prepare in 5 minutes, plus soaking

1 small red eating apple, ends trimmed

1 small ripe pear, pointy end trimmed

50 g (2 oz) gluten-free rolled oats

400 ml (14 fl oz) unsweetened almond milk, plus extra to taste

25 g (1 oz) chopped almonds

125 g (4 oz) fresh blackberries

To serve

mixed seeds

maple syrup or honey

Using a spiralizer fitted with a 3 mm (⅛ inch) spaghetti blade, spiralize the apple and pear.

Place all the remaining ingredients in a large bowl, add the spiralized fruit and stir until combined. Cover and leave to soak in the refrigerator for 2–3 hours, or overnight, to allow the oats to absorb the liquid.

Stir before serving and add a little extra milk, if a runnier consistency is preferred. Serve sprinkled with seeds and drizzled with maple syrup or honey.

There is no need to pre-cook the sweet potato as the steam in the waffle maker will cook it through.

sweet potato waffles with fresh fruit

Using a spiralizer fitted with a 3 mm (⅛ inch) spaghetti blade, spiralize the sweet potato.

In a large bowl, beat together the egg, buttermilk, melted butter or oil, flour, cinnamon and baking powder and whisk together. Stir in the spiralized sweet potato.

Preheat a waffle machine according to the manufacturer's instructions and spray with oil or brush with a little butter. Divide the batter between the 2 waffle plates, being careful not to overfill them, then cook for 5–6 minutes, until golden and cooked through.

Serve immediately with fresh fruit and a drizzle of maple syrup or honey.

Makes 2
Prepare in 5 minutes
Cook in 5–6 minutes

1 sweet potato, about 250 g (8 oz), peeled, ends trimmed and halved widthways

1 large egg, lightly beaten

100 ml (3½ fl oz) buttermilk

1 tablespoon melted butter or coconut oil

2 tablespoons buckwheat flour

1 teaspoon ground cinnamon

½ teaspoon gluten-free baking powder

cooking spray oil or melted butter, for cooking

To serve

fresh fruit, such as blueberries or raspberries

maple syrup or honey

Perfect for brunch, these potato scones are so simple to make and excellent topped with scrambled eggs.

easy pan-fried potato scones

Serves 2

Prepare in 5 minutes

Cook in 6–8 minutes

1 floury potato, about 250 g (8 oz), peeled and ends trimmed

50 g (2 oz) plain flour, plus extra for dusting

¼ teaspoon baking powder

25 g (1 oz) unsalted butter, melted, plus extra for greasing

salt and freshly ground black pepper

Using a spiralizer fitted with a 3 mm (⅛ inch) spaghetti blade, spiralize the potato. Place the spiralized potato in a food processor and pulse until it resembles rice.

Place the flour, baking powder and salt and pepper in a bowl, add the potato rice and butter and combine gently with a spoon or your hands to make a dough.

Gently shape the dough into 2 balls using lightly floured hands, then transfer to a lightly floured surface. Roll out each ball into a circle about 5 mm (¼ inch) thick and prick all over with a fork.

Heat a frying pan over a medium heat. When hot, carefully smear with a little butter, add the potato scones and cook for 3–4 minutes on each side or until golden brown.

Serve immediately with the topping of your choice.

These deliciously moist muffins can be served warm or cold. They will keep for up to 3–4 days in an airtight container.

pumpkin and oat breakfast muffins

Line a muffin tin with 10 paper muffin cases.

Using a spiralizer fitted with a 3 mm (⅛ inch) spaghetti blade, spiralize the pumpkin or squash. Roughly snip any long spirals into shorter lengths with scissors.

In a large bowl, sift together the flour and baking powder. Stir in the oats and spices and mix well. In a separate bowl, beat together the eggs, buttermilk, maple syrup or honey and oil. Pour over the dry ingredients and stir until just combined, then stir in the spiralized pumpkin or squash.

Divide the mixture between the muffin cases, then sprinkle the tops with the pumpkin seeds. Bake in a preheated oven, 190°C (375°F), Gas Mark 5, for 20–25 minutes, until risen and firm.

Makes 10
Prepare in 10 minutes
Cook in 20–25 minutes

large chunk of peeled pumpkin or butternut squash (the non-bulbous end), about 300 g (10 oz)

200 g (7 oz) wholemeal flour

1 tablespoon baking powder

125 g (4 oz) rolled oats

½ teaspoon ground ginger

½ teaspoon ground cinnamon

2 eggs

175 ml (6 fl oz) buttermilk

4 tablespoons maple syrup or honey

3 tablespoons coconut or sunflower oil

2 tablespoons pumpkin seeds

If you prefer, you can top these sweetcorn and courgette cakes with some crispy bacon.

sweetcorn and courgette cakes

Serves 2
Prepare in 5 minutes
Cook in 6–10 minutes

1 corn on the cob

1 courgette, ends trimmed and halved widthways

4 spring onions, thinly sliced

3 tablespoons self-raising flour

2 eggs, beaten

1 tablespoon sunflower oil, for frying

salt and freshly ground black pepper

For the smashed avocado

1 large ripe avocado

juice of ½ lime

2 tablespoons chopped fresh coriander

½ red chilli, deseeded and finely chopped

Hold the corn upright on a chopping board and, using a large sharp knife, carefully slice the kernels off the cob. Heat a griddle or frying pan over a high heat. Add the corn and cook for 2–3 minutes, until blackened slightly, then transfer to a large bowl.

Using a spiralizer fitted with a 3 mm (⅛ inch) spaghetti blade, spiralize the courgette. Roughly snip any really long spirals in half with scissors.

Add the spiralized courgette to the corn with the spring onions, flour and eggs. Season with salt and plenty of pepper, then mix well.

Heat a little oil in a large nonstick frying pan over a medium heat. Add large spoonfuls of the batter (to make 4 cakes) and cook for 2–3 minutes on each side, until lightly browned and cooked through.

Meanwhile, halve, stone, peel and roughly chop the avocado. Place in a bowl with the lime juice, coriander and chilli and smash together with a fork to roughly combine. Season to taste.

Place 2 cakes on each plate and serve immediately, topped with the smashed avocado.

Instead of potatoes you can use a selection of vegetables, such as parsnips or swede.

sausage and egg breakfast traybake

Serves 2
Prepare in 5 minutes
Cook in 25 minutes

2 large potatoes, skins scrubbed, ends trimmed and halved widthways

1 tablespoon olive oil

4 pork sausages

6 mini portabellini mushrooms

2 smoked back bacon rashers

2 tomatoes, halved

2 large eggs

salt and freshly ground black pepper

tomato or brown sauce, to serve

Using a spiralizer fitted with a 6 mm (¼ inch) flat noodle blade, spiralize the potatoes.

Place the spiralized potatoes in a large bowl, add 2 teaspoons of the oil, season with salt and pepper and toss well to coat in the oil and seasoning. Spread out the potatoes in a large, shallow nonstick roasting tin.

Bake in a preheated oven, 200°C (400°F), Gas Mark 6, for 5 minutes, then add the sausages and mushrooms and drizzle the remaining oil over the mushrooms. Return to the oven and bake for a further 10 minutes, turning the sausages and potatoes halfway through the cooking time. Add the bacon and tomatoes to the tin and bake for a further 5 minutes, until the potatoes are crispy and sausages cooked through. Using the back of a spoon, make 2 holes in the potatoes. Crack an egg into each and season with salt and pepper. Return to the oven and bake for 3–4 minutes, until the eggs are softly set.

Carefully divide the mixture between 2 plates and serve immediately with tomato or brown sauce.

courgetti egg rolls with smoked salmon and avocado

Using a spiralizer fitted with a 3 mm (⅛ inch) spaghetti blade, spiralize the courgette. Roughly snip any extra-long spirals in half with scissors. Place the spiralized courgette on a clean tea towel or kitchen paper and gently squeeze out any excess liquid.

In a small jug, lightly beat together the eggs with salt and pepper.

Heat a small nonstick frying pan over a medium heat and spray or brush with oil. Add half the spiralized courgette and stir-fry for 1 minute, then pour over half the eggs and swirl the pan to coat the base. Cook for 2–3 minutes, until the base is set, then flip over the omelette and cook for a further 1 minute, until set.

Meanwhile, halve, stone and peel the avocado and cut into strips.

Slide the omelette on to a board, add half the smoked salmon or trout and avocado and roll up. Serve immediately. Repeat with the remaining ingredients to make 2 egg rolls.

Serves 2
Prepare in 5 minutes
Cook in 8–10 minutes

1 courgette, ends trimmed and halved widthways

3 eggs

cooking spray oil or a little sunflower oil, for frying

1 ripe avocado

4 slices smoked salmon or trout, cut into strips

salt and freshly ground black pepper

This spicy breakfast dish, invented during the days of the Raj, makes a perfect weekend breakfast or a simple supper dish.

smoked haddock and sweet potato kedgeree

Serves 2
Prepare in 10 minutes
Cook in 10–12 minutes

1 sweet potato, about 300 g (10 oz), peeled, ends trimmed and halved widthways

1 small onion, ends trimmed

2 teaspoons sunflower oil

15 g (½ oz) butter

1 tablespoon gluten-free mild or medium curry paste

200 g (7 oz) boneless, skinless smoked haddock, cut into small chunks

75 g (3 oz) frozen peas

juice of ½ lemon

2 eggs

2 tablespoons chopped flat leaf parsley

salt and freshly ground black pepper

lemon wedges, to serve

Using a spiralizer fitted with a 3 mm (⅛ inch) spaghetti blade, spiralize the sweet potato. You should end up with about 250 g (8 oz) spiralized sweet potato.

Place the spiralized sweet potato in a food processor and pulse until it resembles rice.

Spiralize the onion and snip the spirals into 5–6 cm (2–2½ inch) lengths with scissors.

Heat the oil and butter in a large nonstick frying pan or wok with a lid over a medium heat. Add the spiralized onion and cook for 2–3 minutes, until softened. Stir in the sweet potato rice and curry paste and cook for a further 2 minutes, stirring to coat the rice in the paste. Stir in the haddock, peas and lemon juice, cover and cook over a low heat for 5–6 minutes, until the fish is cooked through and the sweet potato rice is tender.

Meanwhile, bring a small saucepan of water to the boil, add the eggs and cook for 4 minutes. Drain, leave to cool slightly and then shell the eggs.

Stir the parsley into the kedgeree and season to taste with salt and pepper. Cut the eggs into quarters.

Divide the kedgeree between 2 plates and top with the eggs. Serve immediately with lemon wedges to squeeze over.

This colourful hash make a great weekend breakfast or brunch, full of health-giving nutrients.

beetroot, onion and sweet potato hash

(gf)

Serves 2
Prepare in 10 minutes
Cook in 15–20 minutes

1 red onion, ends trimmed

1 sweet potato, peeled, ends trimmed and halved widthways

1 fresh beetroot, scrubbed and ends trimmed

2 teaspoons olive oil

125 g (4 oz) chorizo, diced

2 eggs

pinch of smoked paprika

1 tablespoon chopped flat leaf parsley

salt and freshly ground black pepper

Using a spiralizer fitted with a 3 mm (⅛ inch) spaghetti blade, spiralize the onion, keeping it separate. Change to a 6 mm (¼ inch) flat noodle blade and spiralize the sweet potato and beetroot.

Heat 1 teaspoon of the oil in a large nonstick frying pan or wok with a lid over a medium heat. Add the chorizo and spiralized onion and cook for 2–3 minutes, until the onion has softened and the paprika oil has been released from the chorizo. Remove from the pan.

Add the remaining oil to the pan, stir in the spiralized beetroot and sweet potato and stir-fry for 2–3 minutes, then cover and steam for 3–4 minutes, until just tender. Season to taste with salt and pepper.

Return the chorizo and onion to the pan and mix well. Cook, uncovered, for 2–3 minutes, without stirring, until the bottom is lightly browned. Turn over the mixture and cook for a further 2–3 minutes. Using the back of a spoon, make 2 holes in the mixture. Crack in the eggs, cover and cook for 3–4 minutes, until the eggs are just set.

Sprinkle over the paprika and parsley and serve immediately.

If you don't have the Yorkshire pudding tins you can use nonstick muffin tins – just cook the mixture for about 5 minutes more.

mini bacon, tomato and ricotta frittatas

Lightly oil 6 nonstick Yorkshire pudding tins, each about 10 cm (4 inches) in diameter.

Heat the oil in a frying pan over a medium heat. Add the bacon and cook for 3–4 minutes, until lightly browned. Drain on kitchen paper.

Meanwhile, using a spiralizer fitted with a 3 mm (⅛ inch) spaghetti blade, spiralize the courgette. Place the spiralized courgette on a clean tea towel or kitchen paper and gently squeeze out any excess liquid. Roughly snip any really long spirals in half with scissors.

In a large bowl, beat together the eggs and chives and season with salt and pepper. Add the spiralized courgette and the bacon and stir well.

Divide the mixture between the prepared tins, dot each with the ricotta and add 2 tomato halves to each tin. Bake in a preheated oven, 180°C (350°F), Gas Mark 4, for 15 minutes, until set. Serve the frittatas warm. Any leftovers can be stored for up to 2–3 days in an airtight container in the refrigerator.

Makes 6
Prepare in 10 minutes
Cook in 20 minutes

1 teaspoon olive oil, plus extra for greasing

3 smoked back bacon rashers, rind removed and chopped

1 courgette, ends trimmed and halved widthways

6 eggs

1 tablespoon chopped chives

50 g (2 oz) ricotta cheese

6 cherry or baby plum tomatoes, halved

salt and freshly ground black pepper

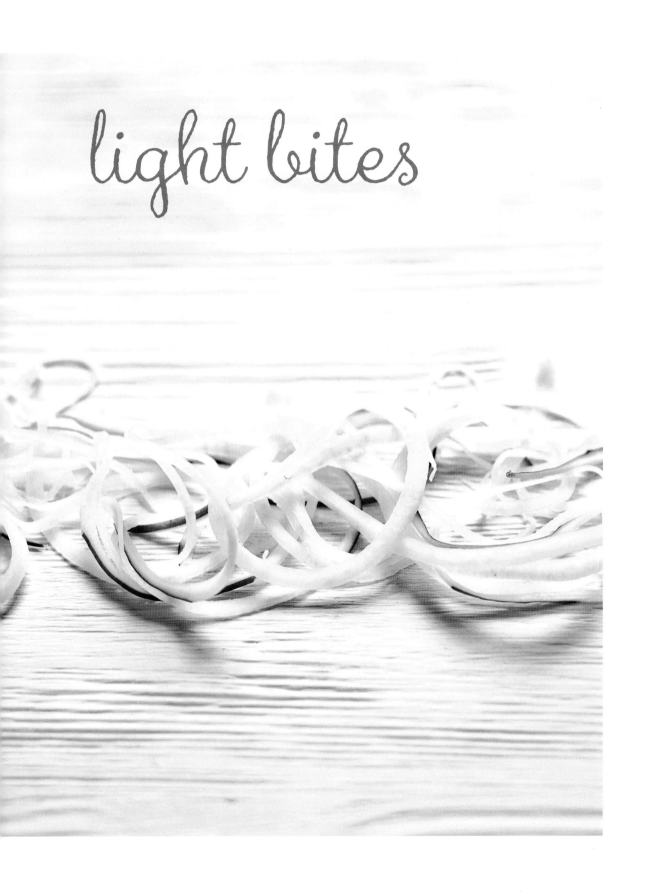

light bites

Pho, pronounced 'fuh' not 'fo', is probably Vietnam's most famous dish. This fragrant soup is perfect for a light meal.

Vietnamese chicken pho with daikon noodles

Serves 2
Prepare in 10 minutes
Cook in 25 minutes

2 teaspoons sunflower oil

1 teaspoon black peppercorns

1 lemon grass stalk, trimmed and sliced

½ cinnamon stick

1 star anise

2.5 cm (1 inch) piece fresh root ginger, peeled and thinly sliced

600 ml (1 pint) hot gluten-free chicken stock

400 ml (14 fl oz) boiling water

1 boneless, skinless chicken breast

275 g (9 oz) piece daikon, peeled, ends trimmed and halved widthways

½ carrot, peeled and ends trimmed

2 teaspoons gluten-free Thai fish sauce

juice of 1 lime

3 spring onions, thinly shredded

½ fat red chilli, deseeded and very thinly sliced

a small handful of coriander leaves

2 lime wedges, to serve

Heat the oil in a large saucepan, add the peppercorns, lemon grass, cinnamon, star anise and ginger and cook for 1–2 minutes to release their aromas. Add the stock, measurement water and chicken breast. Bring to the boil, then cover and simmer for 20 minutes or until the chicken is cooked through.

Meanwhile, using a spiralizer fitted with a 3 mm (⅛ inch) spaghetti blade, spiralize the daikon and carrot, keeping them separate. You should end up with about 250 g (8 oz) spiralized daikon.

Remove the chicken from the stock and set aside. Strain the stock through a sieve into a jug and return to the pan. Shred the chicken using 2 forks, then add to the stock. Stir in the fish sauce, lime juice, spiralized daikon and the spring onions and cook for 3 minutes or until the noodles are tender.

Divide the pho between 2 bowls and scatter with the chilli, spiralized carrot and the coriander. Serve immediately with lime wedges to squeeze over.

For a vegetarian soup, just omit the crispy bacon garnish and top with a little crumbled vegetarian cheese.

celeriac and apple soup with bacon

Serves 2
Prepare in 5 minutes
Cook in 15–20 minutes

1 onion, ends trimmed

500 g (l lb) celeriac, peeled and cut into 12 cm (5 inch) chunks

1 tablespoon olive oil

15 g (½ oz) butter

2 eating apples, ends trimmed

1 small thyme sprig

750 ml (1 ¼ pints) hot gluten-free vegetable stock

salt and freshly ground black pepper

For the crispy bacon garnish

1 teaspoon olive oil

2 smoked back bacon rashers, chopped

6 sage leaves

Using a spiralizer fitted with a 3 mm (⅛ inch) spaghetti blade, spiralize the onion and celeriac, keeping them separate.

Heat the oil and butter in a saucepan, add the spiralized onion and cook over a low heat for 2–3 minutes, until softened.

Meanwhile, spiralize the apples using the 3 mm (⅛ inch) spaghetti blade.

Add the spiralized celeriac and apples to the pan and cook for 2 minutes, then add the thyme and stock. Bring to the boil, then reduce the heat, cover and simmer for 10–12 minutes, until the celeriac and apples are softened.

Carefully pour three-quarters of the soup into a large jug, then purée with a stick blender, until smooth. Stir into the soup in the pan, heat through and season to taste.

Meanwhile, make the garnish. Heat the oil in a frying pan over a medium heat, add the bacon and cook until coloured, then stir in the sage leaves and cook until crispy.

Ladle the soup into 2 bowls and serve topped with the crispy bacon and sage.

Make your own sushi using vegetable rice – I've chosen daikon, but the rolls would also work well with carrot or beetroot rice.

salmon, avocado and daikon rice nori rolls

Line a small baking sheet with kitchen paper.

Using a spiralizer fitted with a 3 mm (⅛ inch) spaghetti blade, spiralize the daikon. Place in a food processor and pulse until it resembles rice. Spread out the daikon rice on the prepared baking sheet, place another piece of kitchen paper over the top and press down to absorb any excess liquid.

Place the mayonnaise and wasabi paste in a bowl, mix together and season to taste with salt and pepper. Stir in the daikon rice.

Stone and peel the avocado, then cut into thin slices.

Place a sheet of nori on a bamboo mat, shiny-side down. Spread half of the daikon rice mixture evenly over the nori, leaving a border of about 2.5 cm (1 inch) on the top edge. Arrange half the salmon slices over the rice, then top with half the avocado slices in a single layer. Roll up the nori tightly from the bottom edge, using the mat to help form a tight roll. Place on a board, seam-side down. Repeat with the remaining ingredients to make 2 rolls.

Trim the ends of the rolls, then using a wet knife, slice each into 6 pieces. Serve with pickled ginger, extra wasabi and soy sauce.

Makes 12
Prepare in 15 minutes

250 g (8 oz) piece daikon, peeled, ends trimmed and halved widthways

2 tablespoons gluten-free light mayonnaise

1 teaspoon wasabi paste, plus extra to serve

½ ripe avocado

2 nori (dried seaweed) sheets

125 g (4 oz) smoked salmon, cut into strips

salt and freshly ground black pepper

To serve
gluten-free pickled ginger
gluten-free soy sauce

This thin and crispy pizza is a great way of getting the kids to eat extra vegetables.

cauliflower-crust Mediterranean pizza

Serves 2

Prepare in 10 minutes

Cook in 20–25 minutes

For the base

550 g (1 lb 2 oz) cauliflower florets

1 teaspoon dried oregano

½ teaspoon garlic salt

25 g (1 oz) vegetarian pasta cheese or Parmesan cheese, grated

1 egg, beaten

salt and freshly ground black pepper

For the topping

½ courgette, ends trimmed

2 tablespoons sundried tomato paste

25 g (1 oz) mozzarella cheese, grated

½ yellow pepper, cored, deseeded and diced

6 cherry tomatoes, halved

75 g (3 oz) soft goats' cheese, roughly chopped

basil leaves

Place a large nonstick baking sheet in a preheated oven, 200°C (400°F), Gas Mark 6.

Place the cauliflower in a food processor and pulse until it resembles rice. Transfer to a microwavable bowl, cover with clingfilm and pierce the top, then cook on full power in a microwave for 4 minutes, until tender. (Alternatively, cook in a steamer over a pan of boiling water.) Leave to cool slightly, then place in a clean tea towel and squeeze over a sink to remove the excess liquid. Return to the bowl and add the oregano, garlic salt, vegetarian pasta cheese or Parmesan, egg and salt and pepper and mix well.

Transfer the mixture to a piece of nonstick baking paper. Using your hands, flatten into a thin circle, about 22 cm (9 inch) in diameter, then carefully transfer to the hot baking sheet. Bake for 12–15 minutes, until golden brown.

Meanwhile, using a spiralizer fitted with a ribbon blade, spiralize the courgette.

Spread the tomato paste over the base and sprinkle over the mozzarella. Top with the spiralized courgette, yellow pepper and tomatoes, then dot over the goats' cheese.

Return the pizza to the oven and bake for 5–7 minutes or until the vegetables are cooked through and the cheese is melted. Scatter over the basil and serve immediately.

These Moroccan-style patties can be served with a crisp green salad as well as the creamy yogurt dip.

beetroot, chickpea and rose harissa patties

Serves 2
Prepare in 10 minutes
Cook in 8–10 minutes

1 fresh beetroot, about 200 g (7 oz), scrubbed and ends trimmed

1 x 400 g (13 oz) can chickpeas, drained and rinsed

2 tablespoons olive oil, plus extra for frying

2 teaspoons rose harissa paste

2 teaspoons tahini paste

2 teaspoons ground cumin

2 tablespoons roughly chopped fresh coriander

2 tablespoons buckwheat flour

salt and freshly ground black pepper

For the dip

4 tablespoons Greek yogurt

2 tablespoons chopped mint

1 teaspoon pomegranate molasses

½ teaspoon rose harissa paste

Using a spiralizer fitted with a 3 mm (⅛ inch) spaghetti blade, spiralize the beetroot.

Place the chickpeas in a food processor with the olive oil, harissa and tahini pastes, cumin and coriander and blitz to a smooth paste. Add the spiralized beetroot and pulse a few times until the beetroot has broken down slightly.

Transfer the chickpea and beetroot mixture to a bowl, add the flour and mix well. Season with salt and pepper and shape the mixture into 4 thick patties.

To make the dip, mix together all the ingredients in a bowl, season to taste and set aside.

Heat a little olive oil in a large frying pan over a medium heat. Add the patties and cook for 4–5 minutes on each side, until golden brown and crisp. Serve the patties with the yogurt dip.

If you prefer, you can make 8 smaller patties and cook for just 3–4 minutes on each side.

These Indian-inspired fritters are delicious served with a cooling cucumber dip or mango chutney.

spicy carrot and coriander fritters

Using a spiralizer fitted with a 3 mm (⅛ inch) spaghetti blade, spiralize the carrots and onion.

In a large bowl, mix together the flour, baking powder, spices and salt. Stir in the eggs and buttermilk or yogurt to make a smooth batter. Add the spiralized vegetables, the garlic and coriander and mix until combined.

Heat a little of the oil in a large nonstick frying pan over a medium heat. Cooking 4 fritters at a time, add heaped tablespoons of the batter to the pan, flatten slightly and cook for 3 minutes on each side, until golden. Repeat until all the batter is used up. Serve the fritters with a cucumber dip and lemon wedges to squeeze over.

Makes about 6
Prepare in 10 minutes
Cook in 15 minutes

200 g (7 oz) carrots, peeled, ends trimmed and halved widthways

1 small onion, ends trimmed

50 g (2 oz) gram flour

1 teaspoon gluten-free baking powder

1 teaspoon ground cumin

1 teaspoon garam masala

½ teaspoon ground turmeric

½ teaspoon salt

2 eggs, lightly beaten

100 ml (3½ fl oz) buttermilk or natural yogurt

1 garlic clove, crushed

2 tablespoons chopped fresh coriander

1 tablespoon olive or sunflower oil, for frying

To serve
cucumber dip
lemon wedges

smoky black bean, chipotle and vegetable quesadilla

Serves 2–3
Prepare in 5 minutes
Cook in 6–8 minutes

1 carrot, peeled, ends trimmed and halved widthways

½ courgette, ends trimmed

150 g (5 oz) canned black beans, drained

2 tablespoons chipotle sauce

2 large soft flour tortillas

2 spring onions, chopped

50 g (2 oz) canned sweetcorn

75 g (3 oz) mozzarella cheese, grated

2 teaspoons olive oil

mixed salad, to serve

Using a spiralizer fitted with a 3 mm (⅛ inch) spaghetti blade, spiralize the carrot and courgette.

In a small bowl, mash the beans with the chipotle sauce.

Lay out 1 tortilla on a board and spread with the black bean mixture, then top with the spiralized vegetables and scatter over the spring onions, sweetcorn and cheese. Place the remaining tortilla on top and press down.

Brush a large frying or griddle pan with the oil and heat. When hot, add the quesadilla and cook over a medium heat for 3–4 minutes, pressing down with a spatula until the cheese starts to melt and the underneath is golden.

Place a large plate over the pan and carefully invert the pan to turn the quesadilla on to the plate. Return to the pan and cook on the other side for 3–4 minutes, until golden.

Transfer the quesadilla to a board, cut into wedges and serve with a mixed salad.

kohlrabi carpaccio with Parma ham and Parmesan cheese

Using a spiralizer fitted with a ribbon blade, spiralize the kohlrabi.

Arrange the spiralized kohlrabi on a large plate, then squeeze over the lemon juice and drizzle with the oil. Sprinkle with a little sea salt, some pepper and the thyme and then leave to marinate for about 1 hour.

Just before you are ready to serve, using a potato peeler, shave over the Parmesan and arrange the ham over the top. Divide between 2 plates and serve immediately.

Serves 2 as a starter

Prepare in 5 minutes, plus marinating

1 small kohlrabi, peeled and ends trimmed

½ lemon

2 teaspoons olive oil

a few small lemon thyme sprigs

25 g (1 oz) piece Parmesan cheese

4 slices Parma ham or prosciutto

sea salt and freshly ground black pepper

This Thai-style salad is hot, fruity and fragrant. It also works well with cooked peeled prawns.

spicy crab and green papaya lettuce wraps

Serves 4

Prepare in 15 minutes, plus marinating

1 small green papaya, about 450 g (14½ oz), peeled and ends trimmed

1 carrot, peeled, ends trimmed and halved widthways

4 spring onions, finely sliced

200 g (7 oz) white crab meat

2 tablespoons chopped fresh coriander

12 large Little Gem leaves

For the dressing

1 passion fruit

juice of 1 lime

1 teaspoon palm or soft brown sugar

2 teaspoons finely grated ginger

1 teaspoon gluten-free fish sauce

½–1 red chilli, deseeded and finely chopped

Cut the papaya in half widthways and tap out the seeds. Attach the narrow end of one half of the papaya to a spiralizer fitted with a 3 mm (⅛ inch) spaghetti blade and spiralize. Repeat with the remaining papaya half. Place the spiralized papaya in a large bowl. Spiralize the carrot and add to the bowl with the spring onions.

To make the dressing, halve the passion fruit and, using a teaspoon, scoop out the pulp into a small bowl. Add all the remaining dressing ingredients, adding the chilli to taste, and stir until the sugar has dissolved.

Add the crab to the papaya mixture and pour over half the dressing. Toss well and leave to marinate for about 10 minutes, stirring halfway through the marinating time. Stir in the coriander.

Place the lettuce leaves on a large plate and spoon in the papaya and crab mixture. Serve immediately with the remaining dressing in a small bowl to spoon over.

This Asian-inspired tuna salad is fresh and zingy and makes a perfect lunch or light evening meal.

griddled tuna with carrot and cucumber salad

Serves 2

Prepare in 15 minutes, plus marinating

Cook in 4–6 minutes

2 x 175 g (6 oz) tuna steaks, about 2.5 cm (1 inch) thick

½ cucumber, ends trimmed and halved widthways

1 carrot, peeled, ends trimmed and halved widthways

2 Little Gem lettuces, ends trimmed and each cut into quarters

4 spring onions, thinly sliced

2 teaspoons toasted sesame seeds

For the marinade

finely grated rind and juice of 2 unwaxed limes

4 tablespoons gluten-free soy sauce

1 garlic clove, crushed

2 teaspoons freshly grated ginger

1 teaspoon sesame oil

2 teaspoons light brown sugar

In a small bowl, mix together the marinade ingredients and stir until the sugar has dissolved. Pour half into a shallow non-reactive dish, reserving the remainder in a bowl to use as a dressing. Add the tuna to the dish and turn to coat in the marinade, then leave to marinate for about 15 minutes.

Meanwhile, using a spiralizer fitted with a 3 mm (⅛ inch) spaghetti blade, spiralize the cucumber and carrot.

Place the spiralized vegetables in a bowl with the lettuce and spring onions.

Heat a griddle pan over a high heat. Remove the tuna from the marinade, add to the pan and cook for 2–3 minutes on each side or until the outside is cooked but the middle is still pink, brushing with any remaining marinade from the dish.

Pour the reserved dressing in the bowl over the carrot and cucumber salad. Toss well, then divide between 2 plates. Top the salad with the tuna steaks, sprinkle with the sesame seeds and serve immediately.

This spicy warming soup can be adapted to add whatever vegetables you have left over.

winter vegetable and red lentil soup

Using a spiralizer fitted with a 3 mm (⅛ inch) spaghetti blade, spiralize all the vegetables, keeping the onion separate.

Heat the oil in a saucepan, add the spiralized onion and cook over a low heat for 3–4 minutes, until softened. Stir in the chilli and cumin and cook for 1 minute, then stir in the lentils.

Add the stock and bring to the boil, then reduce the heat, cover and simmer for 15 minutes, stirring occasionally, until the lentils are tender. Add all the remaining spiralized vegetables and simmer for a further 4–5 minutes or until the soup has thickened and the vegetables are tender. Season to taste.

Ladle the soup into bowls and serve with a dollop of yogurt and the coriander.

Serves 2–3

Prepare in 10 minutes

Cook in 25 minutes

1 onion, ends trimmed

1 sweet potato, peeled, ends trimmed and halved widthways

1 carrot, peeled, ends trimmed and halved widthways

1 parsnip, peeled, ends trimmed and halved widthways

1 tablespoon sunflower oil

1 red chilli, deseeded and chopped

1 tablespoon ground cumin

50 g (2 oz) red lentils, rinsed in cold water and drained

750 ml (1 ¼ pints) hot gluten-free vegetable stock

salt and freshly ground black pepper

To serve

Greek yogurt

chopped fresh coriander

This salad can be served as a light lunch; for a more substantial meal serve with some warm bread, if you like.

courgette, tomato and mozzarella salad

Serves 4

Prepare in 10 minutes, plus marinating

2 courgettes, ends trimmed and halved widthways

300 g (10 oz) cherry or baby plum tomatoes, halved

25 g (1 oz) pitted black olives

1 x 250 g (8 oz) ball buffalo mozzarella cheese, drained

25 g (1 oz) pine nuts, toasted

12 basil leaves

For the dressing

1 garlic clove, crushed

1 teaspoon aged balsamic vinegar

1 teaspoon capers, chopped

juice of 1 lemon

2 tablespoons olive oil

freshly ground black pepper

Using a spiralizer fitted with a ribbon blade, spiralize the courgettes. Roughly snip any extra-long ribbons in half with a pair of scissors.

Place the spiralized courgettes in a large bowl and add the tomatoes and olives.

To make the dressing, whisk together all the dressing ingredients in a small bowl. Pour the dressing over the salad, reserving a little, then leave to marinate for about 10 minutes.

Place the courgettes, tomatoes and olives on a platter. Tear the mozzarella into pieces and arrange over the salad, then scatter over the pine nuts and basil leaves. Drizzle with the remaining dressing and serve immediately.

These crispy strings will remind you of Twiglets, and are perfect for munching on as a snack or with drinks.

Marmite and cheese potato strings

Line a large baking sheet with nonstick baking paper.

Using a spiralizer fitted with a 3 mm (⅛ inch) spaghetti blade, spiralize the potatoes. Roughly snip the spirals into 12–15 cm (5–6 inch) lengths with scissors.

Place the spiralized potatoes in a large bowl, add 2 teaspoons of the oil and season with a little pepper. Toss the strings to coat in the oil and seasoning.

Spread out the spiralized potatoes in a single layer on the prepared baking sheet and bake in a preheated oven, 200°C (400°F), Gas Mark 6, for 10 minutes.

Meanwhile, in a large bowl, mix together the Marmite, remaining oil and the cheese.

Remove the strings from the oven and toss in the Marmite mixture, stirring until evenly coated. Return to the oven and bake for a further 10–12 minutes, until crispy, turning once. (Remove any strings that are already cooked when you turn over the potatoes.) Remove from the oven and leave to cool. The strings can be stored for up to 2–3 days in an airtight container.

Serves 4 as a snack

Prepare in 5 minutes

Cook in 20–22 minutes

2 potatoes, skins scrubbed and ends trimmed

1 tablespoon sunflower oil

1 tablespoon Marmite or yeast extract

25 g (1 oz) mature Cheddar cheese, finely grated

freshly ground black pepper

This pretty salad combines crunch from the apples and fennel with tangy blue cheese.

apple, fennel and Gorgonzola salad

First, make the dressing. In a small bowl, whisk together all the dressing ingredients and season to taste with a little salt and pepper.

Using a spiralizer fitted with a ribbon blade, spiralize the fennel and apples. Snip any really long ribbons into shorter lengths with scissors.

Place the spiralized fennel and apples in a bowl and pour over half the dressing. Add the radishes and toss gently to coat.

Divide the pea shoots between 4 plates or arrange on a platter, then add the apple and fennel mixture. Scatter over the walnuts, cheese and chopped fennel tops. Drizzle over the remaining dressing and serve immediately.

(gf) (lc)

Serves 4
Prepare in 10 minutes

1 large fennel bulb, ends trimmed and leafy tops chopped

1 large red eating apple, ends trimmed

1 large green eating apple, ends trimmed

125 g (4 oz) radishes, thinly sliced

75 g (3 oz) pea shoots

50 g (2 oz) walnut halves

125 g (4 oz) Gorgonzola cheese, broken into small pieces

For the dressing

2 tablespoons extra virgin olive oil

2 tablespoons cider vinegar

2 teaspoons gluten-free wholegrain mustard

2 teaspoons honey

salt and freshly ground black pepper

This hearty soup, flavoured with warming spices, is perfect for an autumnal or winter's day meal.

spiced butternut squash, potato and chorizo soup

Serves 4
Prepare in 10 minutes
Cook in 20 minutes

1 large onion, ends trimmed

1 potato, peeled and ends trimmed

½ butternut squash (the non-bulbous end), about 500 g (1 lb), peeled and halved widthways

1 tablespoon olive oil

½ teaspoon ground cinnamon

1 teaspoon ground ginger

pinch of ground nutmeg

750 ml (1 ¼ pints) hot gluten-free chicken or vegetable stock

125 g (4 oz) chorizo, diced

salt and freshly ground black pepper

1 tablespoon chopped chives, to garnish

Using a spiralizer fitted with a 3 mm (⅛ inch) spaghetti blade, spiralize the onion, keeping it separate. Change to a 6 mm (¼ inch) flat noodle blade and spiralize the potato and squash.

Heat the oil in a large saucepan, add the spiralized onion and cook over a medium heat for 3–4 minutes, stirring occasionally, until softened. Stir in the spiralized potato and squash, cover and cook for 3 minutes.

Stir in the spices and cook for 1 minute, then pour over the stock. Cover and simmer for 10 minutes or until the potatoes and squash are tender. Transfer half the soup to a food processor or blender and blend in batches until smooth. Return to the pan and reheat gently. Season to taste with salt and pepper.

Meanwhile, heat a nonstick frying pan over a medium heat, add the chorizo and cook for 2–3 minutes, stirring occasionally, until the paprika oil has been released from the chorizo and it is crispy.

Ladle the soup into 4 bowls, top with the chorizo and chives and serve immediately.

These crunchy courgette and cheese crisps make a great snack or accompaniment to a glass of wine.

oven-baked courgette and cheese crisps

Line 2 large baking sheets with nonstick baking paper.

Using a spiralizer fitted with a ribbon blade, spiralize the courgette. Snip the spirals into 7.5 cm (3 inch) lengths with scissors.

Place the polenta, vegetarian pasta cheese or Parmesan and pepper in a bowl and mix together until well combined. In a separate small bowl, whisk the egg whites with a fork until frothy. Place the spiralized courgettes, a few at a time, in the egg whites and turn to coat, then place in the cheese mixture and gently shake until completely coated in the mixture.

Transfer the courgettes to the prepared baking sheets, leaving a small space between each spiral. Sprinkle over any remaining cheese mixture and bake in a preheated oven, 200°C (400°F), Gas Mark 6, for 12–15 minutes, turning once, until crispy. Serve immediately.

Serves 2

Prepare in 10 minutes

Cook in 12–15 minutes

1 courgette, ends trimmed and halved widthways

50 g (2 oz) fine polenta (cornmeal)

50 g (2 oz) vegetarian pasta cheese or Parmesan cheese, finely grated

2 egg whites

freshly ground black pepper

chicken with beetroot rice, pomegranate and pistachio tabbouleh

(gf) (lc)

Serves 2

Prepare in 15 minutes, plus marinating

Cook in 8–12 minutes

2 teaspoons grated unwaxed orange rind

4 tablespoons orange juice

2 tablespoons olive oil

2 tablespoons pomegranate molasses

2 boneless, skinless chicken breasts

2 fresh beetroot, scrubbed and ends trimmed

4 tablespoons chopped flat leaf parsley

4 tablespoons chopped mint

50 g (2 oz) baby kale or spinach

100 g (3½ oz) pomegranate seeds

25 g (1 oz) pistachios

salt and freshly ground black pepper

In a large non-reactive bowl, mix together half of the orange rind, orange juice, oil and pomegranate molasses, add the chicken breasts and leave to marinate for about 15 minutes.

Meanwhile, using a spiralizer fitted with a 3 mm (⅛ inch) spaghetti blade, spiralize the beetroot. Place the spiralized beetroot in a food processor and pulse until it resembles rice.

Tip the beetroot rice into a large bowl and stir in the herbs, kale or spinach, pomegranate seeds and pistachios.

In a separate small bowl, mix together the remaining orange rind, orange juice, oil and pomegranate molasses. Season to taste with salt and pepper and then pour over the beetroot tabbouleh and toss well.

Heat a griddle pan until hot. Add the chicken and cook over a medium heat for 4–6 minutes on each side or until cooked through, basting occasionally.

Divide the tabbouleh between 2 bowls. Thinly slice the chicken, arrange over the top and serve immediately.

This Korean dish is made by fermenting Chinese leaves, carrot and daikon. It's a great accompaniment to meat and fish dishes.

easy spiralized vegetable kimchi

Makes 1 x 1 litre (1¾ pint) jar

Prepare in 15 minutes, plus overnight standing and fermenting

1 small head of Chinese leaves, quartered lengthways and cut into 2.5 cm (1 inch) strips

2 tablespoons sea salt

2 carrots, peeled, ends trimmed and halved widthways

150 g (5 oz) piece daikon, peeled, ends trimmed and halved widthways

4 spring onions, chopped

For the kimchi paste

2.5 cm (1 inch) piece fresh root ginger, peeled and grated

2 garlic cloves, crushed

4 tablespoons rice vinegar

1 tablespoon gluten-free Thai fish sauce

2 tablespoons gluten-free sriracha chilli sauce or chilli paste

1 teaspoon caster sugar

Place the Chinese leaves in a bowl, add the sea salt and mix together. Leave to stand for 4–5 hours or overnight.

Using a spiralizer fitted with a 3 mm (⅛ inch) spaghetti blade, spiralize the carrots and daikon.

Place the spiralized vegetables in a large bowl with the spring onions. Rinse the Chinese leaves under cold running water, drain and dry thoroughly, then add to the bowl.

To make the kimchi paste, place all the ingredients in a small bowl and blend together. Stir the paste into the vegetables until evenly coated.

Pack the vegetable mixture into a large jar or freezer box, seal and leave to ferment at room temperature overnight. Transfer to the refrigerator and use within 2 weeks. The flavour will improve the longer it's left.

Use golden beetroot if you can find it – if you use red beetroot, it will stain the pickle red.

mixed vegetable ribbon pickle

Serves 4

Prepare in 10 minutes, plus salting and marinating

1 carrot, peeled, ends trimmed and halved widthways

1 cucumber, ends trimmed and cut into 4 pieces widthways

1 fresh golden beetroot, scrubbed and ends trimmed

125 g (4 oz) radishes, thinly sliced

2 tablespoons sea salt flakes

200 ml (7 fl oz) white wine vinegar

75 g (3 oz) caster sugar

100 ml (3½ fl oz) water

1 teaspoon yellow mustard seeds

2 teaspoons fennel seeds

4 tablespoons roughly chopped dill

Using a spiralizer fitted with a ribbon blade, spiralize the carrot, cucumber and beetroot.

Place the spiralized vegetables in a colander standing over a bowl, add the radishes and sprinkle over the salt. Toss to combine and leave to stand for 20 minutes. Rinse under cold running water, then drain well.

Place the vinegar, sugar and measurement water in a large jar or non-reactive bowl and stir until the sugar has dissolved. Add the mustard and fennel seeds and dill. Stir in the drained vegetables and seal the jar or cover the bowl. Chill in the refrigerator for at least 20 minutes before serving.

These pretty pickled cucumber spirals are quick to prepare and make an ideal accompaniment to cold meats or cheese.

pickled cucumber and dill spirals

Using a spiralizer fitted with a ribbon blade, spiralize the cucumber. Dry the spiralized cucumber on kitchen paper.

Place the vinegar, measurement water, sugar and salt in a non-reactive bowl and whisk together until the sugar and salt have dissolved. Stir in the dill, garlic and peppercorns.

Place the spiralized cucumber in a 750 ml (1 ¼ pint) pickling jar, with a lid. Pour the vinegar mixture over the cucumber and stir well.

Seal the jar and leave in the refrigerator for at least 1 day before serving. The pickled cucumber will keep for up to a few weeks in the refrigerator.

Serves 6–8

Prepare in 10 minutes, plus 1 day pickling

1 cucumber, ends trimmed and cut into 4 pieces widthways

150 ml (¼ pint) white wine vinegar

300 ml (½ pint) warm water

1 teaspoon caster sugar

2 teaspoons sea salt

25 g (1 oz) dill, roughly chopped

4 garlic cloves, peeled and smashed

1 teaspoon black peppercorns

mains

The dumplings are served on a bed of carrot and courgette spaghetti with a tangy chilli and lime dressing.

Asian steamed chicken dumplings

Serves 2

Prepare in 15 minutes

Cook in 15 minutes

2 courgettes, ends trimmed and halved widthways

1 carrot, peeled, ends trimmed and halved widthways

2 tablespoons toasted peanuts, roughly chopped

finely grated rind and juice of 1 unwaxed lime

6 tablespoons gluten-free sweet chilli sauce

½ teaspoon gluten-free Thai fish sauce

For the dumplings

2 spring onions, roughly chopped

2.5 cm (1 inch) piece fresh root ginger, peeled and chopped

1 red chilli, deseeded and chopped

1 small bunch of fresh coriander

1 large boneless, skinless chicken breast, about 200 g (7 oz), cut into chunks

1 teaspoon gluten-free light soy sauce

First, make the dumplings. Place the spring onions, ginger, chilli and coriander in a food processor and blitz until finely chopped. Add the chicken and soy sauce and pulse again until combined. Transfer the mixture to a bowl and shape into 12 small balls, using wet hands.

Place the dumplings in a steamer over a pan of simmering water and steam for about 15 minutes or until cooked through.

Meanwhile, using a spiralizer fitted with a 3 mm (⅛ inch) spaghetti blade, spiralize the courgettes and carrot.

Place the spiralized vegetables in a bowl with the peanuts. Mix together the lime rind and juice, sweet chilli sauce and fish sauce in a separate small bowl, then pour over the courgettes and carrot, reserving a little. Stir well to coat the vegetables in the dressing.

Divide the vegetables between 2 plates and top with the chicken dumplings. Pour over the reserved dressing and serve immediately.

baked salmon, potato and fennel parcels

Serves 2

Prepare in 10 minutes

Cook in 15 minutes

1 large potato, skin scrubbed, ends trimmed and halved widthways

½ fennel bulb, ends trimmed

2 teaspoons olive oil

1 tablespoon chopped parsley

6 pitted black olives

8 capers

6 plum or cherry tomatoes, halved

4 lemon wedges

2 skinless salmon fillets, about 200 g (7 oz) each

salt and freshly ground black pepper

Using a spiralizer fitted with a 3 mm (⅛ inch) spaghetti blade, spiralize the potato and fennel. Roughly snip any really long spirals of potato in half with scissors.

Transfer the spiralized vegetables to a bowl, add the oil and parsley, season well with salt and pepper and mix together.

Place 2 x 23 cm (9 inch) squares of baking paper on a large baking sheet. Divide the potato and fennel mixture, olives, capers, tomatoes and lemon wedges between the 2 sheets of baking paper and then place a salmon fillet on top of each pile of vegetables. Fold over the paper to seal the parcels.

Place the baking sheet in a preheated oven, 200°C (400°F), Gas Mark 6, for 15 minutes, until the salmon is opaque and flakes easily and the potatoes are tender. Transfer the parcels to plates, carefully open the baking paper and squeeze over the lemon wedges. Serve immediately.

beetroot, quinoa and feta burgers with yogurt and harissa

Using a spiralizer fitted with a 3 mm (⅛ inch) spaghetti blade, spiralize the beetroot and carrot. Roughly snip any long spirals in half with scissors.

Place the spiralized vegetables in a bowl, add the quinoa, walnuts, mint, lemon juice, harissa paste, flour and feta and stir together. Mix in the egg and season well with salt and pepper. Transfer the mixture to a plate, cover and chill in the refrigerator for 30 minutes.

Divide the mixture into 4 portions and shape into burgers, using your hands. Place the burgers on a nonstick baking sheet and brush with a little oil. Cook the burgers under a preheated hot grill for 6–7 minutes on each side or until cooked through.

Top the burgers with spoonfuls of yogurt drizzled with the harissa and serve with salad leaves and tomatoes.

Makes 4

Prepare in 10 minutes, plus chilling

Cook in 12–15 minutes

1 fresh beetroot, scrubbed and ends trimmed

1 carrot, peeled, ends trimmed and halved widthways

125 g (4 oz) cooked quinoa

50 g (2 oz) chopped walnuts

4 tablespoons chopped mint

juice of ½ lemon

2 teaspoons harissa paste

2 tablespoons wholemeal flour

125 g (4 oz) feta cheese, crumbled

1 large egg, beaten

salt and freshly ground black pepper

1 tablespoon sunflower oil, for brushing

To serve

Greek yogurt

1 teaspoon harissa paste

mixed salad leaves and tomatoes

Biryani is traditionally a rice dish. Here I have replaced the rice with low-carb cauliflower rice, which absorbs the spices well.

vegetable biryani with cauliflower rice

(gf) (lc) (v) (vg)

Serves 4
Prepare in 10 minutes
Cook in 10 minutes

550 g (1 lb 2 oz) cauliflower florets

1 small onion, ends trimmed

1 large carrot, peeled, ends trimmed and halved widthways

1 courgette, ends trimmed and halved widthways

1 tablespoon sunflower oil

2 teaspoons black mustard seeds

5 cardamom pods, crushed

2 tablespoons gluten-free medium curry powder

1 cinnamon stick

6 curry leaves

2.5 cm (1 inch) piece fresh root ginger, peeled and finely grated

1 green chilli, deseeded and finely chopped

1 garlic clove, crushed

150 ml (¼ pint) hot gluten-free vegetable stock or water

2 tomatoes, chopped

salt and freshly ground black pepper

To serve

2 tablespoons chopped fresh coriander

25 g (1 oz) toasted almonds

Place the cauliflower in a food processor and pulse until it resembles rice. Set aside.

Using a spiralizer fitted with a 3 mm (⅛ inch) spaghetti blade, spiralize the onion, keeping it separate. Change to a ribbon blade and spiralize the carrot and courgette. Roughly snip any long ribbons in half with scissors.

Heat the oil in a large frying pan or wok over a medium heat. Stir in the spices and curry leaves and cook for 1 minute or until the mustard seeds start to pop. Stir in the spiralized onion, the ginger, chilli, garlic and 2 tablespoons of the stock or water and cook for 3–4 minutes, until the onion has softened.

Add the cauliflower rice and stir to coat in the spices, then add the spiralized carrot and courgette and the tomatoes. Stir well, then pour in the remaining stock or water. Cook for 5 minutes or until the liquid has evaporated and the rice and vegetables are tender, stirring occasionally. Season to taste with salt and pepper.

Divide the biryani between 4 bowls and scatter with the coriander and almonds. Serve immediately.

smoked salmon, courgette and dill crustless quiche

Serves 4
Prepare in 10 minutes
Cook in 35–40 minutes

1 courgette, ends trimmed and halved widthways

1 tablespoon sunflower oil, plus extra for greasing

4 eggs

300 ml (½ pint) reduced-fat crème fraîche, plus extra to serve

150 g (5 oz) smoked salmon, cut into strips

75 g (3 oz) reduced-fat mature Cheddar cheese, grated

2 tablespoons chopped dill, plus extra sprigs to garnish

salt and freshly ground black pepper

watercress, to serve

Using a spiralizer fitted with a ribbon blade, spiralize the courgette. Snip any extra-long ribbons into shorter lengths with scissors.

Place the spiralized courgette in a bowl and toss in the oil. Heat a large griddle pan until hot. Add the courgette in a single layer and cook for 2–3 minutes, until lightly charred – you may need to do this in 2 batches. Transfer the courgette to a plate lined with kitchen paper and leave to cool.

Lightly grease a 20 cm (8 inch) nonstick cake tin and line the base with baking paper.

In a large bowl, lightly beat together the eggs and crème fraîche and then lightly season with salt and pepper. Add half the salmon and courgette ribbons, 50 g (2 oz) of the cheese and the dill.

Pour into the prepared tin, top with the remaining courgettes and salmon and sprinkle over the remaining cheese. Bake in a preheated oven, 180°C (350°F), Gas Mark 4, for 30–35 minutes or until the filling is just set. Remove from the oven and leave to cool slightly.

Cut the quiche into wedges, garnish with dill sprigs and serve with large handfuls of watercress.

These cheesy carrot tortillas are lower in carbs than traditional wheat flour tortillas.

carrot tortillas with chipotle chicken

Line 2 large baking sheets with nonstick baking paper.

First, make the tortillas. Using a spiralizer fitted with a 3 mm (⅛ inch) spaghetti blade, spiralize the carrots. Place the spiralized carrots in a steamer over a pan of boiling water and steam for 3 minutes, until just tender. Leave to cool slightly, then place the carrots on a clean tea towel or kitchen paper and gently squeeze out any excess liquid.

Tip the carrots into a bowl, stir in all the remaining tortilla ingredients and season well. Place 4 large spoonfuls of the mixture on to the prepared baking sheets and, using the back of a spoon, press out into thin circles about 15 cm (6 inches) in diameter. Bake in a preheated oven, 200°C (400°F), Gas Mark 6, for 10 minutes, until golden and crispy on the edges.

Meanwhile, heat the oil in a wok or large frying pan. Add the chicken and stir-fry for 3–4 minutes, until browned. Add the onion and peppers and stir-fry for 2–3 minutes, then add the tomatoes and chipotle paste. Simmer for 5 minutes or until the sauce is thick and glossy, adding more chipotle paste to taste, if liked.

Divide the chipotle chicken between the warm tortillas, scatter with the coriander, roll up and serve immediately.

Serves 2
Prepare in 15 minutes
Cook in 15 minutes

2 teaspoons sunflower oil

2 small boneless, skinless chicken breasts, cut into thin strips

1 small red onion, sliced

½ red pepper, deseeded and cut into thin strips

½ yellow pepper, deseeded and cut into thin strips

1 x 227 g (8 oz) can chopped tomatoes

1 tablespoon chipotle paste, or to taste

2 tablespoons chopped fresh coriander

For the tortillas

2 large carrots, peeled, ends trimmed and halved widthways

2 eggs, beaten

75 g (3 oz) Cheddar cheese, grated

2 tablespoons almond flour

salt and freshly ground black pepper

tiger prawns with daikon noodles and Asian pesto

Serves 2
Prepare in 10 minutes
Cook in 4–6 minutes

1 daikon, about 375 g (12 oz), peeled, ends trimmed and halved widthways

1 tablespoon groundnut oil

200 g (7 oz) raw peeled tiger prawns

For the pesto

1 lemon grass stalk, tough outer layers removed and roughly chopped

1 small red chilli, deseeded and roughly chopped

finely grated rind and juice of 1 unwaxed lime

25 g (1 oz) fresh coriander

12 basil leaves

2.5 cm (1 inch) piece fresh root ginger, peeled and chopped

1 garlic clove

25 g (1 oz) gluten-free dry-roasted peanuts

2 tablespoons groundnut oil

1 teaspoon gluten-free Thai fish sauce

First, make the pesto. Place all the pesto ingredients except the oil and fish sauce in a food processor and blitz to make a paste – you may need to scrape the mixture down the sides of the food processor with a rubber spatula from time to time. With the motor still running, gradually add the oil and fish sauce through the funnel until combined. Set aside.

Using a spiralizer fitted with a 3 mm (⅛ inch) spaghetti blade, spiralize the daikon.

Heat the oil in a large wok or frying pan, add the prawns and cook for 2–3 minutes, until they have turned pink. Add the spiralized daikon and stir-fry for 2–3 minutes, until just tender. Stir in the pesto and toss well to coat the daikon noodles and prawns. Serve immediately.

If you prefer, you can just stir this nutrient-packed creamy sauce into raw courgetti.

courgetti with herby avocado sauce

Using a spiralizer fitted with a 3 mm (⅛ inch) spaghetti blade, spiralize the courgettes.

Halve, stone and peel the avocado, then place in a food processor with the garlic, lemon juice, herbs and olive or avocado oil and blitz until smooth. Season to taste with salt and pepper.

Spray the base of a nonstick frying pan or wok with spray oil and heat over a medium heat. Add the spiralized courgettes and stir-fry for 3–4 minutes, until just tender. Remove from the heat and stir in the sauce to coat.

Divide the courgetti between 2 bowls, sprinkle with the pine nuts and extra pepper and serve immediately.

(gf) (lc) (v) (vg)

Serves 2
Prepare in 10 minutes
Cook in 5 minutes

2 courgettes, ends trimmed and halved widthways

1 ripe avocado

1 garlic clove

juice of ½ lemon

4 tablespoons roughly chopped flat leaf parsley

25 g (1 oz) basil leaves

2 tablespoons olive or avocado oil

cooking spray oil, for frying

25 g (1 oz) pine nuts, toasted

salt and freshly ground black pepper

Give this classic Chinese dish a low-carb makeover by swapping egg noodles with carrot and daikon noodles.

chicken chow mein with vegetable noodles

In a large bowl, mix together 1 tablespoon each of the soy sauce, sherry or Chinese cooking wine and oyster sauce, the sesame oil and 1 teaspoon of the cornflour. Add the chicken, stir to coat in the marinade, then cover and leave to marinate in the refrigerator for 20 minutes.

In a small bowl, mix together the remaining soy sauce, sherry or Chinese cooking wine, oyster sauce and cornflour and set aside.

Using a spiralizer fitted with a 6 mm (¼ inch) flat noodle blade, spiralize the carrot, keeping it separate. Change to a 3 mm (⅛ inch) spaghetti blade and spiralize the daikon.

Heat the sunflower oil in a wok or large frying pan over a high heat until hot. Add the chicken and stir-fry for 3–4 minutes, until lightly browned. Add the garlic, ginger and spring onions and stir-fry for 2–3 minutes. Add the spiralized vegetables and the mangetout and stir-fry for a further 3–4 minutes, until the vegetables are just tender and the chicken is cooked through. Add the bean sprouts and reserved sauce and stir until the sauce has thickened and coated all the ingredients. Serve immediately.

Serves 4

Prepare in 10 minutes, plus marinating

Cook in 10–15 minutes

2 tablespoons gluten-free light soy sauce

2 tablespoons dry sherry or Chinese cooking wine (Shaoxing)

3 tablespoons gluten-free oyster sauce

½ teaspoon toasted sesame oil

2 teaspoons cornflour

3 boneless, skinless chicken breasts, cut into thin strips

1 large carrot, peeled, ends trimmed and halved widthways

1 daikon, about 500 g (1 lb), peeled, ends trimmed and halved widthways

1 tablespoon sunflower oil

1 garlic clove, crushed

2 teaspoons grated fresh root ginger

1 bunch of spring onions, sliced

125 g (4 oz) mangetout

125 g (4 oz) bean sprouts

This Bolognese will become a family favourite and is packed full of vegetables and flavour.

skinny turkey Bolognese with courgetti

Serves 4

Prepare in 10 minutes

Cook in 25–35 minutes

3 courgettes (ideally yellow courgettes), ends trimmed and halved widthways

1 large onion, ends trimmed

1 large carrot, peeled, ends trimmed and halved widthways

450 g (14½ oz) lean minced turkey

1 garlic clove, crushed

250 g (8 oz) closed cup or chestnut mushrooms, sliced

1 teaspoon paprika

150 ml (¼ pint) red wine or gluten-free beef stock

1 x 400 g (13 oz) can chopped tomatoes

1 tablespoon tomato purée

2 teaspoons dried mixed herbs

salt and freshly ground black pepper

freshly grated Parmesan cheese, to serve

Using a spiralizer fitted with a 3 mm (⅛ inch) spaghetti blade, spiralize the courgettes and onion, keeping them separate. Change to a ribbon blade and spiralize the carrot. Roughly snip any really long ribbons in half with scissors.

Place the mince, spiralized onion and garlic in a large nonstick saucepan and dry-fry over a high heat for 3–4 minutes, until lightly browned. Stir in the spiralized carrot, mushrooms and paprika and cook for 2–3 minutes. Stir in the red wine or stock and cook for 2–3 minutes, until the liquid has reduced, then stir in the tomatoes, tomato purée and mixed herbs. Reduce the heat, cover and simmer for 15–20 minutes, stirring occasionally, until the sauce has reduced and thickened.

Season to taste with salt and pepper, then stir in the spiralized courgettes and cook, uncovered, for 2–3 minutes or until the courgettes are al dente. Serve sprinkled with a little Parmesan.

fennel and cauliflower risotto with lemon and rocket

Serves 2

Prepare in 10 minutes

Cook in 10–15 minutes

1 fennel bulb, ends trimmed and reserved

250 g (8 oz) cauliflower florets

1 tablespoon olive oil

1 garlic clove, crushed

½ red chilli, deseeded and finely chopped (optional)

100 ml (3½ fl oz) white wine

200 ml (7 fl oz) hot gluten-free vegetable stock

finely grated rind and juice of 1 small unwaxed lemon

50 g (2 oz) vegetarian pasta cheese or Parmesan cheese, grated, plus extra to serve

2 tablespoons reduced-fat cream cheese

50 g (2 oz) rocket leaves

salt and freshly ground black pepper

Using a spiralizer fitted with a 6 mm (¼ inch) flat noodle blade, spiralize the fennel.

Cut the trimmed ends of the fennel into small pieces and place in a food processor with the spiralized fennel and cauliflower florets. Pulse until the mixture resembles rice.

Heat the oil in a large frying pan or wok, add the garlic and chilli, if using, and cook over a medium heat for 1 minute, until softened, then add the cauliflower and fennel rice. Stir-fry for 2–3 minutes, then pour in the wine and cook for 2–3 minutes until the liquid has reduced. Add half the stock and cook until most of the stock has evaporated. Stir in the remaining stock and half of the lemon rind and juice and season with salt and pepper. Cook for a further 2–3 minutes, until the rice is just tender.

Stir in the vegetarian pasta cheese or Parmesan, cream cheese and most of the rocket, reserving a little. Cook for a further 1–2 minutes or until the rocket has wilted and the rice is tender. Stir in the remaining lemon rind and juice.

Divide the risotto between 2 bowls, top with the reserved rocket and sprinkle with extra vegetarian pasta cheese or Parmesan and pepper. Serve immediately.

Make this crowd pleaser into a low-carb meal with daikon noodles and plenty of vegetables.

sweet and sour pork with daikon noodles

Using a spiralizer fitted with a 6 mm (¼ inch) flat noodle blade, spiralize the carrot. Change to a 3 mm (⅛ inch) spaghetti blade and spiralize the daikon. Set the vegetables aside.

Drain the pineapple and pour the juice into a small bowl, reserving the pineapple pieces. Add all the sauce ingredients, except the cornflour, to the pineapple juice and mix well. Place the cornflour in a cup, then blend with 2 tablespoons of the sauce, stirring until smooth. Stir the cornflour mixture into the sauce in the bowl.

Heat the oil in a wok or large frying pan, add the pork, ginger and garlic and stir-fry over a high heat for 3–4 minutes, until browned. Add the spiralized vegetables, red pepper, spring onions and reserved pineapple pieces and cook for a further 2–3 minutes, until the vegetables are tender and the pork is cooked through.

Pour the sauce mixture into the pan, bring to the boil, stirring continuously, and simmer for 2–3 minutes, until thickened. Serve immediately.

Serves 4
Prepare in 15 minutes
Cook in 8–12 minutes

1 carrot, peeled, ends trimmed and halved widthways

1 daikon, about 500 g (1 lb), peeled, ends trimmed and halved widthways

1 x 227 g (8 oz) can pineapple pieces, in natural juice

2 teaspoons sunflower oil

450 g (14½ oz) pork fillet, cut into small cubes

2 teaspoons grated fresh root ginger

1 garlic clove, crushed

1 red pepper, cored, deseeded and cubed

1 bunch of spring onions, sliced

For the sauce

1 tablespoon gluten-free tomato ketchup

1 tablespoon tomato purée

1 tablespoon gluten-free light soy sauce

2 tablespoons rice wine vinegar

1 tablespoon cornflour

butternut squash spaghetti with walnut and rocket pesto

(gf) (lc) (v)

Serves 4

Prepare in 10 minutes

Cook in 10 minutes

½ large coquina or butternut squash (the non-bulbous end), peeled and cut in half widthways

2 teaspoons olive oil

freshly ground black pepper

For the pesto

75 g (3 oz) rocket leaves, plus extra to garnish

1 garlic clove

50 g (2 oz) walnut halves

4 tablespoons grated vegetarian pasta cheese or Parmesan cheese

juice of ½ lemon

4 tablespoons extra virgin olive oil

First, make the pesto. Place the rocket, garlic, walnuts, vegetarian pasta cheese or Parmesan and lemon juice in a food processor and blitz until finely chopped – you may need to scrape the mixture down the sides of the food processor with a rubber spatula from time to time. With the motor still running, gradually add the oil through the funnel until combined.

Using a spiralizer fitted with a 3 mm (⅛ inch) spaghetti blade, spiralize the squash. You should end up with about 500 g (1 lb) spiralized squash.

Heat the olive oil in a large wok or frying pan, add the spiralized squash and stir-fry for about 5–7 minutes, until softened but not broken up. Stir in the pesto until the squash spaghetti is well coated. Sprinkle with pepper, garnish with a few rocket leaves and serve immediately.

miso-baked cod with daikon noodles and Asian greens

(lc)

Serves 2

Prepare in 15 minutes, plus marinating

Cook in 14–17 minutes

2 chunky cod loins, about 200 g (7 oz) each

sunflower oil, for oiling

250 g (8 oz) piece daikon, peeled, ends trimmed and halved widthways

3 tablespoons black sesame seeds

½ teaspoon caster sugar

1 tablespoon seasoned soy sauce

1 tablespoon liquid dashi

1 teaspoon yuzu juice or lemon juice

300 g (10 oz) choi sum and pak choi, stems trimmed and leaves cut into bite-sized pieces

For the marinade

2 tablespoons white miso paste

3 tablespoons sake

1 garlic clove, crushed

2.5 cm (1 inch) piece fresh root ginger, peeled and finely grated

1 tablespoon caster sugar

2 teaspoons mirin

In a shallow dish, mix together all the marinade ingredients, add the cod and turn to coat in the marinade. Cover and leave to marinate in the refrigerator for 2–3 hours, or overnight

Lightly oil a baking sheet. Using a spiralizer fitted with a 6 mm (¼ inch) flat noodle blade, spiralize the daikon.

Place the fish on the prepared baking sheet and spoon over 1 tablespoon of the marinade. Bake in a preheated oven, 180°C (350°F), Gas Mark 4, for 10–12 minutes.

Preheat the grill to high. Remove the fish from the oven, spoon the remaining marinade over the fish and grill for about 4–5 minutes, until golden brown and cooked through.

Meanwhile, toast the sesame seeds in a dry frying pan for 2–3 minutes. Transfer to a mortar and pestle and grind to nearly a paste, but still retaining some texture. Add the sugar, soy sauce, dashi and citrus juice and grind to incorporate all the flavours.

Place the spiralized daikon and the choi sum and pak choi in a steamer over a pan of boiling water. Steam for 3–4 minutes or until tender.

Divide the daikon noodles and greens between 2 plates and drizzle over the dressing. Top with the cod and serve immediately.

Fresh seasonal vegetables are cooked in a creamy basil sauce to make the perfect spring recipe.

courgetti with prosciutto, asparagus and peas

Serves 2
Prepare in 5 minutes
Cook in 5–7 minutes

2 courgettes, ends trimmed and halved widthways

125 g (4 oz) ricotta cheese

2 tablespoons fresh pesto sauce

250 g (8 oz) asparagus stalks

2 teaspoons olive oil

4 slices prosciutto, chopped

100 g (3½ oz) fresh peas

4 basil leaves, torn

salt and freshly ground black pepper

freshly grated Parmesan cheese, to serve

Using a spiralizer fitted with a 3 mm (⅛ inch) spaghetti blade, spiralize the courgettes. Set aside.

In a small bowl, mix together the ricotta and pesto sauce. Set aside.

Snap the woody ends off the asparagus stalks and discard. Cut off the top 4 cm (1½ inches) of each asparagus stalk and set aside. Finely chop the remaining stalks.

Heat the oil in a large frying pan or wok, add the chopped asparagus stalks and the prosciutto and gently fry for 2–3 minutes or until the prosciutto is crispy.

Meanwhile, bring a small saucepan of lightly salted water to the boil and add the asparagus tips and peas and cook for 3 minutes, until tender. Drain well.

Add the spiralized courgettes to the chopped asparagus and prosciutto and stir-fry for 2–3 minutes, until just tender, then add the asparagus tips and peas and the ricotta and pesto sauce. Stir to coat the vegetables in the sauce.

Divide the courgetti between 2 bowls and sprinkle with the basil, Parmesan and pepper. Serve immediately.

This low-carb paella makes a fantastic recipe for entertaining and can be cooked in no time at all.

seafood paella with butternut squash rice

Using a spiralizer fitted with a 3 mm (⅛ inch) spaghetti blade, spiralize the onion and squash, keeping them separate. Place the spiralized squash in a food processor and pulse until it resembles rice.

Place the saffron in a small bowl, add the measurement water and leave to soak.

Heat the oil in a large frying pan with a lid. Add the chorizo, spiralized onion and garlic and cook over a medium heat for 3–4 minutes, until the paprika oil has been released from the chorizo and the onion has softened. Add the squash rice, saffron water and paprika and cook for 1 minute, then stir in the tomatoes and peas.

Place the cod, prawns and squid rings on top of the rice, cover and cook for 3 minutes. Stir gently, then place the mussels on top, discarding any that are cracked or don't shut when tapped. Re-cover and cook for 2–3 minutes or until all the mussels have opened, the prawns and fish are cooked through and the rice is tender. Discard any mussels that remain closed.

Divide the paella between 4 bowls, sprinkle with the parsley and serve immediately with lemon wedges to squeeze over.

Serves 4
Prepare in 10 minutes
Cook in 8–12 minutes

1 onion, ends trimmed

½ butternut squash (the non-bulbous end), about 450 g (14½ oz), peeled and halved widthways

pinch of saffron threads

1 tablespoon hot water

1 tablespoon olive oil

75 g (3 oz) chorizo, diced

1 garlic clove, crushed

1 teaspoon smoked paprika

1 x 400 g (13 oz) can chopped tomatoes

50 g (2 oz) frozen peas

125 g (4 oz) boneless, skinless cod fillet, cut into 2.5 cm (1 inch) pieces

12 raw peeled king prawns

150 g (5 oz) squid rings

150 g (5 oz) mussels, scrubbed and debearded

2 tablespoons chopped flat leaf parsley, to garnish

lemon wedges, to serve

salmon teriyaki with courgette and sesame noodles

In a shallow non-reactive dish, mix together all the marinade ingredients, then add the salmon fillets, turn to coat and leave to marinate for 15 minutes.

Meanwhile, line a baking sheet with nonstick baking paper. Using a spiralizer fitted with a 6 mm (¼ inch) flat noodle blade, spiralize the courgettes. Set aside.

Place the salmon on the prepared baking sheet and spoon over some of the marinade. Bake in a preheated oven, 200°C (400°F), Gas Mark 6, for 5 minutes. Spoon over the remaining marinade, return to the oven and cook for a further 5–7 minutes, until the salmon is opaque and the fish flakes easily.

Towards the end of the cooking time, heat the sesame oil in a wok or large frying pan, add the spiralized courgettes, edamame beans and sesame seeds and stir-fry for 3–4 minutes, until the courgettes are just tender.

Divide the courgette noodles between 2 plates, place a salmon fillet on top of each and spoon over any remaining sauce from the baking sheet. Serve immediately.

(gf) (lc)

Serves 2

Prepare in 10 minutes, plus marinating

Cook in 10–12 minutes

2 boneless, skinless salmon fillets, about 150 g (5 oz) each

2 courgettes, ends trimmed and halved widthways

2 teaspoons sesame oil

150 g (5 oz) frozen edamame beans

2 teaspoons sesame seeds

For the marinade

2 tablespoons gluten-free dark soy sauce

1 tablespoon mirin or rice wine vinegar

1 tablespoon honey

1 garlic clove, crushed

2 teaspoons finely grated ginger

creamy Marsala mushrooms on parsnip noodles

Serves 2

Prepare in 5 minutes

Cook in 13–15 minutes

2 parsnips, peeled, ends trimmed and halved widthways

1 teaspoon olive oil

15 g (½ oz) butter

1 garlic clove, crushed

250 g (8 oz) mixed mushrooms, such as chestnut and portobello, sliced

3 tablespoons Marsala wine or sherry

3 tablespoons reduced-fat crème fraîche

4 tablespoons water

1 tablespoon chopped tarragon

salt and freshly ground black pepper

Using a spiralizer fitted with a 6 mm (¼ inch) flat noodle blade, spiralize the parsnips.

Heat the oil and butter in a large frying pan. When the butter starts to foam, add the garlic and mushrooms and cook over a high heat for 5–6 minutes, stirring occasionally, until the mushrooms are lightly browned. Stir in the Marsala or sherry, bring to the boil and simmer for 2 minutes. Add the crème fraîche and stir until melted into the sauce.

Stir in the spiralized parsnips and measurement water and cook for a further 5–6 minutes, until just tender, stirring occasionally and adding a little more water if the sauce becomes too dry. Stir in the tarragon and season to taste with salt and pepper. Serve immediately.

Thai green chicken and butternut squash curry

Using a spiralizer fitted with a 6 mm (¼ inch) flat noodle blade, spiralize the butternut squash and courgette, keeping them separate.

Heat the oil in a saucepan, add the Thai green curry paste and cook for 1–2 minutes, stirring constantly. Stir in the chicken and cook for 2–3 minutes, until lightly browned. Add the coconut milk, lemon grass, lime leaves and fish sauce. Bring to the boil, then reduce the heat and simmer for about 8 minutes, until the sauce has reduced slightly.

Stir in the spiralized squash, cover and simmer for 3 minutes, then stir in the spiralized courgette. Cover and simmer for a further 2–3 minutes, until the vegetables are just tender and the chicken is cooked through. Stir in the basil or coriander and serve immediately.

Serves 4
Prepare in 5 minutes
Cook in 18–20 minutes

½ butternut squash (the non-bulbous end), about 500 g (1 lb), peeled and halved widthways

1 courgette, ends trimmed and halved widthways

2 teaspoons groundnut or vegetable oil

2 tablespoons gluten-free Thai green curry paste

3 boneless, skinless chicken breasts, cut into thin strips

1 x 400 ml (14 fl oz) can coconut milk

1 lemon grass stalk, tough outer layers removed and roughly chopped

2 kaffir lime leaves, thinly sliced

2 teaspoons gluten-free fish sauce

handful of Thai basil or coriander leaves

The courgette replaces the pasta in this low-carb meal. If you prefer, you can replace the beef with lean turkey mince.

beef, courgetti and three-cheese lasagne

Serves 4
Prepare in 15 minutes
Cook in 50–55 minutes

4 large courgettes, ends trimmed and halved widthways

1 tablespoon olive oil

1 onion, ends trimmed

1 carrot, peeled, ends trimmed and halved widthways

500 g (1 lb) lean minced beef

1 garlic clove, crushed

100 ml (3½ fl oz) red wine

1 x 400 g (13 oz) can chopped tomatoes

2 tablespoons tomato purée

2 teaspoons dried mixed herbs

350 g (11½ oz) ricotta cheese

75 g (3 oz) Parmesan cheese, grated

250 g (8 oz) mozzarella cheese, sliced

salt and freshly ground black pepper

Line 2 large baking sheets with nonstick baking paper.

Using a spiralizer fitted with a ribbon blade, spiralize the courgettes. Place the spiralized courgettes in a large bowl, add the oil and a little salt and toss to coat in the oil and seasoning.

Spread out the courgettes in a single layer on the prepared baking sheets and bake in a preheated oven, 180°C (350°F), Gas Mark 4, for 20 minutes, turning the courgettes and swapping over the baking sheets in the oven halfway through the cooking time. Remove from the oven and pat dry with kitchen paper. Set aside.

Meanwhile, spiralize the onion and carrot using the 3 mm (⅛ inch) spaghetti blade, keeping them separate.

Place the beef, spiralized onion and garlic in a large saucepan and dry-fry over a medium heat for 3–4 minutes, until the mince is browned. Add the spiralized carrot and pour over the wine. Simmer for 2 minutes, then add the tomatoes, tomato purée and herbs and season with salt and pepper. Bring to the boil, then reduce the heat, cover and simmer for 15 minutes or until the sauce has reduced and is thick.

In a bowl, beat together the ricotta with 50 g (2 oz) of the Parmesan.

To assemble the lasage, place half the beef sauce in the bottom of a 1.2 litre (2 pint) ovenproof dish, add half the courgettes, cover with the mozzarella and then top with the remaining beef and courgettes. Spread the ricotta mixture over the top, then sprinkle over the remaining Parmesan.

Bake in the oven for 30–35 minutes, until golden and bubbling. Leave to stand for 5 minutes before serving.

This lightly spiced Cajun rice dish is easy to make as it is cooked in one pan. This recipe substitutes carrot rice for long-grain rice.

chicken, chorizo and carrot rice jambalaya

Serves 4
Prepare in 10 minutes
Cook in 15–18 minutes

2 large carrots, peeled, ends trimmed and halved widthways

1 onion, ends trimmed

1 teaspoon sunflower oil

100 g (3½ oz) chorizo, chopped

3 boneless, skinless chicken breasts, cut into small cubes

1 tablespoon gluten-free Cajun seasoning

1 red pepper, cored, deseeded and diced

1 green pepper, cored, deseeded and diced

1 x 400 g (13 oz) can chopped tomatoes

50 g (2 oz) frozen peas

6 spring onions, chopped

100 g (3½ oz) cooked peeled prawns

Using a spiralizer fitted with a 3 mm (⅛ inch) spaghetti blade, spiralize the carrots and onion, keeping them separate. Place the spiralized carrots in a food processor and pulse until the mixture resembles rice.

Heat the oil in a large frying pan, add the chorizo and spiralized onion and cook over a medium heat for 3–4 minutes, until the onion has softened and the paprika oil has been released from the chorizo. Add the chicken and Cajun spice and cook for 3–4 minutes, until the chicken is lightly browned. Stir in the peppers and cook for 2 minutes, then add the carrot rice, tomatoes, peas and spring onions, reserving a few spring onions. Stir to combine.

Simmer for 5 minutes, stirring occasionally. Stir in the prawns and cook for 2 minutes, until the vegetables are tender and the chicken is cooked through. Serve sprinkled with the reserved spring onions.

Roasting the butternut squash and cauliflower rice helps intensify the flavours and drive off excess water.

butternut squash and cauliflower cheese

Serves 2

Prepare in 10 minutes

Cook in 15 minutes

large chunk of butternut squash (the non-bulbous end), about 300 g (10 oz), peeled and halved widthways

75 g (3 oz) chorizo, sliced

450 g (14½ oz) cauliflower florets

100 g (3½ oz) light cream cheese

200 ml (7 fl oz) semi-skimmed milk

75 g (3 oz) reduced-fat mature Cheddar cheese, grated

50 g (2 oz) baby spinach

4 cherry tomatoes, halved

salt and freshly ground black pepper

mixed salad leaves, to serve

Using a spiralizer fitted with a 6 mm (¼ inch) flat noodle blade, spiralize the squash. Spread out the spiralized squash in a single layer on a nonstick baking sheet with the chorizo.

Line a large baking sheet with nonstick baking paper. Place the cauliflower in a food processor and pulse until it resembles rice. Spread out the cauliflower rice on the prepared baking sheet.

Place both baking sheets in a preheated oven, 200°C (400°F), Gas Mark 6, for 12 minutes, stirring halfway through, until the cauliflower rice is dried out and starting to crisp and the chorizo is crispy.

Meanwhile, place the cream cheese, milk and half the Cheddar in a saucepan and season with salt and pepper. Stir over a low heat until the mixture is combined.

Stir the squash noodles, chorizo, cauliflower rice and spinach into the cheese mixture and stir gently, until the spinach starts to wilt. Transfer to a 1.2 litre (2 pint) ovenproof dish, sprinkle with the remaining cheese and top with the tomatoes. Place under a preheated hot grill and cook for 3–4 minutes, until golden and bubbling. Serve immediately with a mixed salad.

Sicilian anchovy, lemon, parsley and chilli courgetti

Using a spiralizer fitted with a 3 mm (⅛ inch) spaghetti blade, spiralize the courgettes.

Drain the olive oil from the anchovies into a large frying pan, add the garlic and cook over a medium heat for 1 minute, then add the anchovies. Cook for 2–3 minutes, until the anchovies begin to soften and cook down. Stir in the chilli flakes, if using, the parsley and lemon juice.

Add the spiralized courgettes and mix well. Stir in most of the Parmesan, reserving a little. Cook for 2 minutes, until the courgettes are al dente, then season to taste with pepper.

Divide the courgetti between 2 bowls, sprinkle with the reserved Parmesan and serve immediately with a rocket salad.

Serves 2
Prepare in 5 minutes
Cook in 6 minutes

2 large courgettes, ends trimmed and halved widthways

1 x 50 g (2 oz) can anchovy fillets, in olive oil

1 garlic clove, crushed

pinch of dried chilli flakes (optional)

3 tablespoons chopped flat leaf parsley

juice of 2 small lemons

25 g (1 oz) Parmesan cheese, grated

freshly ground black pepper

rocket salad, to serve

This lightly spiced Cajun rice dish is easy to make as it is cooked in one pan. This recipe substitutes carrot rice for long-grain rice.

chicken, chorizo and carrot rice jambalaya

Serves 4
Prepare in 10 minutes
Cook in 15–18 minutes

2 large carrots, peeled, ends trimmed and halved widthways

1 onion, ends trimmed

1 teaspoon sunflower oil

100 g (3½ oz) chorizo, chopped

3 boneless, skinless chicken breasts, cut into small cubes

1 tablespoon gluten-free Cajun seasoning

1 red pepper, cored, deseeded and diced

1 green pepper, cored, deseeded and diced

1 x 400 g (13 oz) can chopped tomatoes

50 g (2 oz) frozen peas

6 spring onions, chopped

100 g (3½ oz) cooked peeled prawns

Using a spiralizer fitted with a 3 mm (⅛ inch) spaghetti blade, spiralize the carrots and onion, keeping them separate. Place the spiralized carrots in a food processor and pulse until the mixture resembles rice.

Heat the oil in a large frying pan, add the chorizo and spiralized onion and cook over a medium heat for 3–4 minutes, until the onion has softened and the paprika oil has been released from the chorizo. Add the chicken and Cajun spice and cook for 3–4 minutes, until the chicken is lightly browned. Stir in the peppers and cook for 2 minutes, then add the carrot rice, tomatoes, peas and spring onions, reserving a few spring onions. Stir to combine.

Simmer for 5 minutes, stirring occasionally. Stir in the prawns and cook for 2 minutes, until the vegetables are tender and the chicken is cooked through. Serve sprinkled with the reserved spring onions.

pork medallions with creamy apple and cider sauce

Serves 2

Prepare in 5 minutes

Cook in 15–18 minutes

2 parsnips, peeled, ends trimmed and halved widthways

1 red eating apple, ends trimmed

1 tablespoon sunflower oil

15 g (½ oz) butter

250 g (8 oz) pork fillet, cut into 1.25 cm (½ inch) thick slices

200 ml (7 fl oz) medium-dry cider or apple juice

2 tablespoons chopped sage

4 tablespoons crème fraîche

salt and freshly ground black pepper

Using a spiralizer fitted with a 6 mm (¼ inch) flat noodle blade, spiralize the parsnips, keeping them separate. Change to the ribbon blade and spiralize the apple. Roughly snip any really long ribbons in half with scissors.

Heat the oil and butter in a large frying pan with a lid. Add the pork and cook over a high heat for 2–3 minutes on each side, until browned. Add the spiralized parsnips and cook for 2–3 minutes, stirring continuously. Pour over the cider or apple juice and add the sage and spiralized apple. Bring to the boil, then reduce the heat to medium, cover and simmer for 5–6 minutes, until the sauce has reduced, the vegetables are just tender and the pork is cooked through.

Stir in the crème fraîche and simmer for 2 minutes, until heated through. Season to taste with salt and pepper and serve immediately.

Remember to remove the pan from the heat before adding the egg mixture or it will turn into scrambled eggs!

spiralized sweet potato carbonara

Serves 2
Prepare in 10 minutes
Cook in 10 minutes

1 large sweet potato, about 450 g (14½ oz), peeled, ends trimmed and halved widthways

2 eggs

2 tablespoons single cream

50 g (2 oz) Parmesan cheese, grated

1 teaspoon olive oil

125 g (4 oz) cubed smoked pancetta or chopped streaky bacon

2 garlic cloves, crushed

freshly ground black pepper

1 tablespoon chopped flat leaf parsley, to garnish

Using a spiralizer fitted with a 3 mm (⅛ inch) spaghetti blade, spiralize the sweet potato.

Place the spiralized sweet potato in a steamer over a pan of simmering water and cook for 5–6 minutes or until just tender.

Meanwhile, in a small bowl, beat together the eggs, cream and Parmesan and season with pepper.

Heat the oil in a saucepan, add the pancetta or bacon and cook for 2–3 minutes, until crispy. Stir in the garlic and cook for 1 minute. Add the spiralized sweet potatoes and stir to coat in the bacon and garlic mixture, then remove the pan from the heat.

Gently stir in the egg and cheese mixture until everything is well combined. Serve immediately with extra pepper and a sprinkling of parsley.

I have replaced traditional wheat noodles with low-carb daikon noodles in this Japanese-inspired hearty broth.

chilli beef daikon ramen

Using a spiralizer fitted with a 6 mm (¼ inch) flat noodle blade, spiralize the daikon. Set aside.

Place the bean sprouts in a sieve and pour over boiling water, then refresh under cold running water. Set aside.

Place the stock in a large saucepan with the chilli sauce, ginger and garlic, bring to the boil and simmer for 5 minutes.

Meanwhile, brush the steaks with a little oil and season with salt and pepper. Heat a heavy-based frying pan over a high heat until smoking hot. Add the steaks and cook for 2–3 minutes on each side, until browned but still pink in the middle. (Alternatively, cook for 1–2 minutes on each side, if you prefer your steak rare.) Transfer the steaks to a plate, brush over the teriyaki sauce and leave to rest.

Add the mushrooms, pak choi and spiralized daikon to the chilli broth and simmer for 5 minutes, until the vegetables are tender.

Slice the steaks thinly. Divide the daikon noodles between 2 bowls and ladle over the broth. Top each with the steak strips, bean sprouts, spring onions, chilli and coriander. Serve immediately with the lime wedges to squeeze over.

Serves 2
Prepare in 10 minutes
Cook in 10–12 minutes

1 daikon, about 375 g (12 oz), peeled, ends trimmed and halved widthways

125 g (4 oz) bean sprouts

1 litre (1 ¾ pints) hot chicken stock

1 tablespoon hot chilli sauce, or to taste

2.5 cm (1 inch) piece fresh root ginger, peeled and cut into thin matchsticks

1 garlic clove, crushed

2 teaspoons olive oil, for brushing

2 rump or sirloin steaks, about 200 g (7 oz) each, trimmed of fat

2 tablespoons teriyaki sauce

125 g (4 oz) shiitake mushrooms, sliced

200 g (7 oz) pak choi, sliced

3 spring onions, thinly sliced

a few slices red chilli

1 small bunch of fresh coriander

salt and freshly ground black pepper

2 lime wedges, to serve

Spiralizing the squash and making it into rice makes this usually carb-heavy dish into a lighter alternative.

butternut squash and spinach rice-free risotto

Serves 2
Prepare in 10 minutes
Cook in 10–12 minutes

1 small onion, ends trimmed

large chunk of butternut squash (the non-bulbous end), about 375 g (12 oz), peeled and halved widthways

1 tablespoon olive oil

1 garlic clove, crushed

100 ml (3½ fl oz) dry white wine

1 tablespoon chopped sage

200 ml (7 fl oz) hot gluten-free vegetable stock

150 g (5 oz) baby spinach

25 g (1 oz) vegetarian pasta cheese or Parmesan cheese, grated, plus extra to serve

75 g (3 oz) goats' cheese, chopped

salt and freshly ground black pepper

To serve
6 crispy fried sage leaves
25 g (1 oz) pine nuts, toasted

Using a spiralizer fitted with a 3 mm (⅛ inch) spaghetti blade, spiralize the onion and squash, keeping them separate. You should end up with about 350 g (11½ oz) spiralized squash. Place the spiralized squash in a food processor and pulse until it resembles rice.

Heat the oil in a large frying pan, add the spiralized onion and garlic and cook over a medium heat for 2–3 minutes, until softened. Pour in the wine and reduce the liquid by half, then add the squash rice and cook for 2 minutes. Add the chopped sage and half the stock and cook until most of the stock has evaporated. Add the remaining stock, season with salt and pepper and cook for a further 2–3 minutes, until the squash is just tender, adding a little more hot water if needed. Stir in the spinach and vegetarian pasta cheese or Parmesan and stir for about 2 minutes until the spinach has wilted. Stir in the goats' cheese and leave to melt.

Divide the risotto between 2 plates and serve topped with crispy sage leaves, toasted pine nuts and a sprinkling of extra vegetarian pasta cheese or Parmesan.

baking and sweet treats

This cornbread is flecked with chilli and spring onions.
It is very easy to make and contains no yeast.

butternut squash and chilli cornbread

(v)

Makes 6–8 wedges
Prepare in 10 minutes
Cook in 25–30 minutes

2 tablespoons coconut oil or melted butter, plus extra for greasing

large chunk of butternut squash (the non-bulbous end), about 250 g (8 oz), peeled and halved widthways

125 g (4 oz) plain flour

125 g (4 oz) polenta (cornmeal)

2 teaspoons baking powder

1 teaspoon salt

4 spring onions, thinly chopped

1 red chilli, deseeded and finely chopped

2 eggs

250 ml (8 fl oz) buttermilk

Grease a 20 cm (8 inch) springform cake tin and line the base with nonstick baking paper.

Using a spiralizer fitted with a 3 mm (⅛ inch) spaghetti blade, spiralize the squash. Roughly snip any really long spirals in half with scissors.

In a large bowl, mix together the flour, polenta, baking powder, salt, spring onions, chilli and spiralized squash.

In a jug, whisk together the eggs, buttermilk and oil or melted butter and then pour over the dry ingredients. Mix well until all the ingredients are combined.

Pour the mixture into the prepared tin and bake in a preheated oven, 200°C (400°F), Gas Mark 6, for 25–30 minutes, until golden brown, firm and beginning to pull away from the sides of the tin. Remove from the oven and leave to cool slightly in the tin.

Serve warm, sliced or cut into wedges.

sweet banana, butternut squash and pecan loaf

Serves 8–10
Prepare in 10 minutes
Cook in 50–60 minutes

125 g (4 oz) butter, softened, plus extra for greasing

large chunk of butternut squash (the non-bulbous end), about 250 g (8 oz), peeled and halved widthways

150 g (5 oz) soft light brown sugar

2 eggs, lightly beaten

3 ripe bananas, mashed

1 teaspoon vanilla extract

125 g (4 oz) plain flour

125 g (4 oz) wholemeal flour

1 teaspoon bicarbonate of soda

1 teaspoon baking powder

½ teaspoon salt

50 g (2 oz) pecans, roughly chopped, plus 8 to decorate

Grease a 1 kg (2 lb) loaf tin.

Using a spiralizer fitted with a 3 mm (⅛ inch) spaghetti blade, spiralize the squash. Roughly snip any really long spirals in half with scissors.

In a large bowl, cream together the butter and sugar until light and fluffy. Gradually beat in the eggs, bananas and vanilla extract until well combined. Sift in the flours, bicarbonate of soda, baking powder and salt and gently fold in. Stir in the chopped pecans and spiralized squash.

Spoon the mixture into the prepared tin and arrange the pecan halves in a line across the centre. Bake in a preheated oven, 180°C (350°F), Gas Mark 4, for 50–60 minutes or until risen, golden brown and a skewer inserted in the centre comes out clean. Cover the top with foil if it becomes too brown during cooking.

Leave the loaf to cool in the tin for a few minutes, then remove from the tin and transfer to a cooling rack to cool completely before serving.

apple, blackberry and cinnamon crumble muffins

Line a muffin tin with 10 paper muffin cases.

To make the topping, place the flour in a small bowl, add the butter and rub in with the fingertips until the mixture resembles fine breadcrumbs. Stir in the sugar and set aside.

Using a spiralizer fitted with a 6 mm (¼ inch) flat noodle blade, spiralize the apples.

In a large bowl, sift together the flour, baking powder and salt and then stir in the cinnamon and sugar. In a jug, beat together the egg, milk and oil and then pour over the dry ingredients. Mix until just combined and then stir in the spiralized apples and the blackberries. Divide the mixture between the muffin cases and then sprinkle the tops with the crumble topping. Bake in a preheated oven, 190°C (375°F), Gas Mark 5, for 20–25 minutes, until risen and firm.

Makes 10
Prepare in 10 minutes
Cook in 20–25 minutes

2 red eating apples, ends trimmed

300 g (10 oz) plain flour

1 tablespoon baking powder

½ teaspoon salt

1 teaspoon ground cinnamon

125 g (4 oz) caster sugar

1 large egg

200 ml (7 fl oz) milk

75 ml (3 fl oz) sunflower oil

150 g (5 oz) blackberries

For the topping

25 g (1 oz) plain flour

15 g (½ oz) cold butter

2 tablespoons demerara sugar

courgette and Cheddar cheese soda bread

(V)

Makes 1 medium loaf
Prepare in 10 minutes
Cook in 25–30 minutes

1 large courgette, ends trimmed
   and halved widthways

225 g (7½ oz) wholemeal flour

225 g (7½ oz) plain flour, plus
   extra for dusting

½ teaspoon sea salt

1 teaspoon caster sugar

1 teaspoon bicarbonate of soda

75 g (3 oz) mature Cheddar cheese,
   grated

375–400 ml (13–14 fl oz)
   buttermilk, plus extra for
   brushing

Using a spiralizer fitted with a 3 mm (⅛ inch) spaghetti blade, spiralize the courgette. Place the spiralized courgette on a clean tea towel or kitchen paper and gently squeeze out any excess liquid.

Place a large casserole dish and its lid in a preheated oven, 220°C (425°F), Gas Mark 7.

In a large bowl, mix together the spiralized courgette, flours, salt, sugar, bicarbonate of soda and 50 g (2 oz) of the cheese using your hands. Stir in enough of the buttermilk to bring the mixture together to make a soft dough.

Tip the dough out on to a lightly floured surface and knead lightly, then shape into a shallow round loaf about 4 cm (1 ½ inches) thick. Make a cross in the top, brush with a little buttermilk and sprinkle over the remaining cheese.

Carefully remove the hot casserole dish from the oven and dust the inside lightly with flour. Gently lower in the dough, cover with the lid and return to the oven. Bake for about 25–30 minutes, until the loaf is golden and sounds hollow when tapped.

Leave the bread to cool in the dish for 5 minutes, then remove from the dish and transfer to a cooling rack to cool slightly before serving. The bread is best served warm.

The beetroot rice makes these cakes a pretty colour. They are best eaten on the day they are made.

beetroot and vanilla cupcakes

Makes 18

Prepare in 15 minutes, plus cooling

Cook in 18–20 minutes

2 fresh beetroot, scrubbed and ends trimmed

175 g (6 oz) unsalted butter, softened

175 g (6 oz) caster sugar

2 large eggs, beaten

1 tablespoon vanilla extract

175 g (6 oz) self-raising flour

For the frosting

200 g (7 oz) light cream cheese

2 tablespoons icing sugar, sifted

1 tablespoon vanilla extract

Line 1 or 2 bun tins with 18 paper cake cases.

Using a spiralizer fitted with a 3 mm (⅛ inch) spaghetti blade, spiralize the beetroot. Reserving a few spirals for decoration, place the remaining spiralized beetroot in a food processor and pulse until it resembles rice.

In a large bowl, beat together the butter and sugar until light and fluffy. Whisk in the eggs, a little at a time, then whisk in the vanilla extract. Sift in the flour and stir until just combined, then fold in the beetroot rice.

Divide the mixture between the cake cases. Bake in a preheated oven, 180°C (350°F), Gas Mark 4, for 18–20 minutes, until risen and golden brown. Remove from the oven, transfer to a cooling rack and leave to cool completely.

To make the frosting, place all the frosting ingredients in a bowl and beat together until smooth. Spread the frosting over the cooled cakes and decorate with the reserved beetroot spirals.

The addition of spiralized carrots to this gluten-free cake make it deliciously moist.

orange, carrot and almond cake

Serves 8–10

Prepare in 20 minutes, plus cooling

Cook in about 2½ hours

2 unwaxed oranges

butter, for greasing

2 carrots, peeled, ends trimmed and halved widthways

4 eggs

300 g (10 oz) caster sugar

300 g (10 oz) ground almonds

1 teaspoon gluten-free baking powder

4 cardamom pods, seeds crushed

For the syrup

grated rind and juice of 1 unwaxed orange

100 g (3½ oz) caster sugar

2 tablespoons water

1 teaspoon orange blossom water

Place the oranges in a large saucepan and pour over boiling water to cover. Simmer, covered, for 1 hour or until tender. Drain and leave to cool.

Grease a 20 cm (8 inch) springform cake tin and line the base with nonstick baking paper. Using a spiralizer fitted with a 3 mm (⅛ inch) spaghetti blade, spiralize the carrots. Roughly snip any really long spirals in half with scissors.

Cut the cooled oranges in half and remove any pips. Place in a food processor and blitz until smooth.

In a large mixing bowl, whisk together the eggs and sugar with a hand-held electric mixer until thick and pale. Gently fold in the blitzed oranges, the spiralized carrots, reserving a few spirals for decoration, the ground almonds, baking powder and cardamom until combined.

Spoon the mixture into the prepared tin and bake in the centre of a preheated oven, 160°C (325°F), Gas Mark 3, for about 1–1¼ hours or until a skewer inserted in the centre comes out clean. Cover the top with foil if it becomes too brown during cooking. Remove from the oven and leave the cake to cool completely in the tin.

To make the syrup, place the orange juice, sugar and measurement water in a saucepan. Cook over a low heat, stirring, for 5 minutes or until the sugar has dissolved and the syrup thickened slightly. Remove from the heat, stir in the orange blossom water, orange rind and reserved carrot spirals and leave to cool.

Remove the cake from the tin and drizzle over the syrup.

These tasty cookies are made with very little added sugar and are lower in fat than traditional cookies.

sweet potato and chocolate chip cookies

Line 2 large baking sheets with nonstick baking paper.

Using a spiralizer fitted with a 3 mm (⅛ inch) spaghetti blade, spiralize the sweet potato. Place the spiralized sweet potato in a food processor and pulse until it resembles rice.

Place the sweet potato rice in a bowl with the oats, cinnamon or mixed spice and chocolate chips and stir to combine.

In a small bowl, beat together the eggs, almond butter, honey and vanilla extract. Tip into the sweet potato mixture and mix together.

Drop heaped tablespoonfuls of the mixture on to the prepared baking sheets and flatten slightly. Bake in a preheated oven, 180°C (350°F), Gas Mark 4, for 10–12 minutes, until lightly golden.

Remove from the oven and leave the cookies to cool on the sheets for 5 minutes, then transfer to a cooling rack to cool completely. The cookies will keep for up to 2 days in an airtight container.

Makes about 15
Prepare in 10 minutes
Cook in 10–12 minutes

1 sweet potato, about 250 g (8 oz), peeled, ends trimmed and halved widthways

50 g (2 oz) gluten-free rolled oats

½ teaspoon ground cinnamon or mixed spice

75 g (3 oz) gluten-free dark chocolate chips

2 eggs, beaten

3 tablespoons almond butter

1 tablespoon honey

1 teaspoon vanilla extract

The addition of earthy beetroot to these brownie-inspired cookies really intensifies the chocolate flavour.

crackled beetroot brownie cookies

Makes 12–14

Prepare in 10 minutes, plus freezing

Cook in 10–12 minutes

1 fresh beetroot, scrubbed and ends trimmed

50 g (2 oz) cocoa powder

200 g (7 oz) light soft brown sugar

4 tablespoons coconut or sunflower oil

2 eggs

1 teaspoon vanilla extract

125 g (4 oz) plain flour

1 teaspoon baking powder

25 g (1 oz) icing sugar

Using a spiralizer fitted with a 3 mm (⅛ inch) spaghetti blade, spiralize the beetroot. Roughly snip any really long spirals with scissors and place in a large freezerproof bowl.

Place all the remaining ingredients, except the icing sugar, in a food processor and pulse until well combined. Stir the mixture into the spiralized beetroot and freeze for about 30 minutes. Alternatively, you can chill the mixture in the refrigerator for about 2 hours.

Line 2 large baking sheets with nonstick baking paper. Remove the mixture from the freezer and roll into golfball-sized balls. Sift the icing sugar on to a plate, then roll each ball in the icing sugar.

Place the balls well apart on the prepared baking sheets and flatten slightly. Bake in a preheated oven, 180°C (350°F), Gas Mark 4, for 10–12 minutes, until set.

Remove from the oven and leave the cookies to cool on the baking sheets for a few minutes, then transfer to a cooling rack to cool completely. The cookies will keep for up to 2–3 days in an airtight container.

This dessert is so simple to make and looks spectacular. Prepare just before serving to prevent the apples browning.

apple carpaccio with lime and mint sugar

Using a spiralizer fitted with a ribbon blade, spiralize the apples. Arrange over a large platter and squeeze over the lime juice.

Place the sugar, lime rind and mint in a food processor and blitz to make a bright green sugar. Sprinkle over the apples and serve immediately.

Serves 4–6

Prepare in 10 minutes

4 red or pink eating apples, ends trimmed

grated rind and juice of 1 unwaxed lime

2 tablespoons golden caster sugar

2 heaped tablespoons mint leaves

These lovely little puddings are deliciously sticky and moist. Perfect for entertaining.

carrot and ginger steamed puddings

Using a spiralizer fitted with a 3 mm (⅛ inch) spaghetti blade, spiralize the carrot. You should end up with about 150 g (5 oz) spiralized carrot. Roughly snip any long spirals into shorter lengths with scissors.

Grease 4 x 150 ml (¼ pint) metal pudding tins, then spoon 1 tablespoon ginger syrup into the bottom of each.

In a large bowl, beat together the butter and sugar until light and fluffy. Gradually beat in the eggs. Gently fold in the flour, milk, stem ginger and spiralized carrot.

Divide the mixture between the prepared tins, then cover each tin tightly with foil and put into a roasting tin. Pour enough boiling water into the tin to come 2 cm (¾ inch) up the sides of the tins. Bake in a preheated oven, 180°C (350°F), Gas Mark 4, for 30–35 minutes or until a skewer inserted in the centre comes out clean.

Leave the puddings to cool in the tins for 5 minutes, then run a knife around the inside of the tins to loosen. Turn out on to plates and drizzle over extra ginger syrup. Serve immediately with custard or cream.

(V)

Serves 4
Prepare in 10 minutes
Cook in 30–35 minutes

1 large carrot, peeled, ends trimmed and halved widthways

125 g (4 oz) butter, softened, plus extra for greasing

4 tablespoons stem ginger syrup, plus extra to serve

125 g (4 oz) caster sugar

2 eggs, beaten

125 g (4 oz) self-raising flour

2 tablespoons milk

4 pieces stem ginger, finely chopped

custard or cream, to serve

These fluffy waffles could also be served for breakfast with just a drizzle of maple syrup or honey.

apple and blueberry waffles with ice cream

Serves 2

Prepare in 5 minutes

Cook in 5–6 minutes

1 red or green eating apple, ends trimmed

2 tablespoons self-raising flour

1 teaspoon caster sugar

1 egg, lightly beaten

½ teaspoon vanilla extract

50 g (2 oz) blueberries

a little cooking spray oil or melted butter, for cooking

vanilla ice cream, to serve

Using a spiralizer fitted with a 6 mm (¼ inch) flat noodle blade, spiralize the apple.

Place the flour and sugar in a bowl and gradually stir in the egg and vanilla extract to make a smooth batter. Add the spiralized apples and the blueberries and mix gently until combined.

Preheat a waffle machine according to the manufacturer's instructions and spray with oil or brush with a little butter. Divide the batter between the 2 waffle plates, being careful not to overfill them, then cook for 5–6 minutes, until golden and cooked through.

Serve immediately with scoops of vanilla ice cream.

For a grown-up popsicle, add 1 teaspoon of gin or Pimm's to each mould.

cucumber, lemon and mint popsicles

Place the measurement water, lemon juice and sugar in a saucepan. Cook over a low heat, stirring until the sugar has dissolved. Pour into a jug and leave to cool, then stir in the chopped mint.

Using a spiralizer fitted with 3 mm (⅛ inch) spaghetti blade, spiralize the cucumber.

Divide the spiralized cucumber between 8 popsicle moulds, then pour in the lemon and mint mixture to come nearly to the top of the moulds. Add a popsicle stick to each mould and freeze for 3–4 hours or until frozen.

Makes 8

Prepare in 10 minutes, plus cooling and freezing

Cook in 5 minutes

400 ml (14 fl oz) water

juice of 2 large lemons

50 g (2 oz) caster sugar

10 mint leaves, finely chopped

½ cucumber, ends trimmed and halved widthways

green plantain rice pudding with coconut and mango

Serves 2–3
Prepare in 5 minutes
Cook in 15 minutes

2 green plantains (the straightest ones you can find)

1 x 400 ml (14 fl oz) can coconut milk

200 ml (7 fl oz) water

6 green cardamom pods, crushed

2 tablespoons caster sugar

To serve
toasted coconut shavings
fresh chopped mango

Cut the plantains in half widthways. Score the outside of the skins and peel off, then trim the ends. Using a spiralizer fitted with a 3 mm (⅛ inch) spaghetti blade, spiralize the plantains. Place the spiralized plantains in a food processor and pulse until the mixture resembles rice.

Pour the coconut milk into a jug, stir well and then add the measurement water to make up to 600 ml (1 pint).

Place the plantain rice in a saucepan, then stir in 400 ml (14 fl oz) of the coconut milk mixture, the cardamoms and sugar. Bring to the boil, then reduce the heat to low and simmer for 10 minutes, stirring occasionally and adding a little more of the coconut milk if the mixture starts sticking to the bottom of the pan. Add the remaining coconut milk and simmer for a further 2 minutes, until the mixture is creamy and the plantain rice is cooked.

Serve the rice pudding topped with coconut shavings and fresh chopped mango.

dark chocolate and pear crumbles with ice cream

First, make the crumble. Place the flour in a bowl, add the butter and rub in with your fingertips until the mixture resembles fine breadcrumbs. Stir in the remaining crumble ingredients and set aside.

Grease 6 x 250 ml (8 fl oz) ovenproof teacups or ramekins. Using a spiralizer fitted with a 6 mm (¼ inch) flat noodle blade, spiralize the pears.

Place the spiralized pears in a bowl and mix together with the lemon rind and juice, sugar and chocolate. Divide the pear mixture between the prepared teacups or ramekins, spooning over any juice.

Spoon the crumble mixture over the pears and press down lightly. Place the crumbles on a baking sheet and bake in a preheated oven, 180°C (350°F), Gas Mark 4, for 15 minutes, until golden and bubbling. Serve with a spoonful of vanilla ice cream.

Serves 6
Prepare in 15 minutes
Cook in 15 minutes

4 firm pears, pointy ends trimmed

grated rind and juice of 1 unwaxed lemon

50 g (2 oz) light brown soft sugar

50 g (2 oz) dark chocolate chips or chunks

vanilla ice cream, to serve

For the crumble

75 g (3 oz) plain flour

50 g (2 oz) cold butter, diced, plus extra for greasing

50 g (2 oz) rolled oats

50 g (2 oz) light brown soft sugar

50 g (2 oz) dark chocolate chips or chunks

50 g (2 oz) roasted hazelnuts, chopped

This tart is so easy to make and looks impressive. Serve with vanilla ice cream.

spiralized apple puff pastry tart

Serves 6–8
Prepare in 10 minutes
Cook in 15–20 minutes

1 x 320 g (10½ oz) pack ready-rolled puff pastry

2 red or green eating apples, ends trimmed

juice of 1 lemon

50 g (2 oz) butter, diced

3 tablespoons caster sugar

4 tablespoons apricot jam

vanilla ice cream, to serve

Unroll the pastry and place on a nonstick baking sheet. Using a sharp knife, score a 2.5 cm (1 inch) border around the edges, being careful not to cut all the way through.

Using a spiralizer fitted with a ribbon blade, spiralize the apples. Place the spiralized apples in a bowl and toss in the lemon juice.

Dot some of the butter over the pastry and sprinkle with 1 tablespoon of the sugar. Arrange the apples over the pastry, then dot with the remaining butter and sprinkle over the remaining sugar.

Bake in a preheated oven, 220°C (425°F), Gas Mark 7, for 15–20 minutes, until risen, golden and crisp.

Warm the apricot jam in a small saucepan, then brush over the apples and pastry. Serve immediately with scoops of vanilla ice cream.

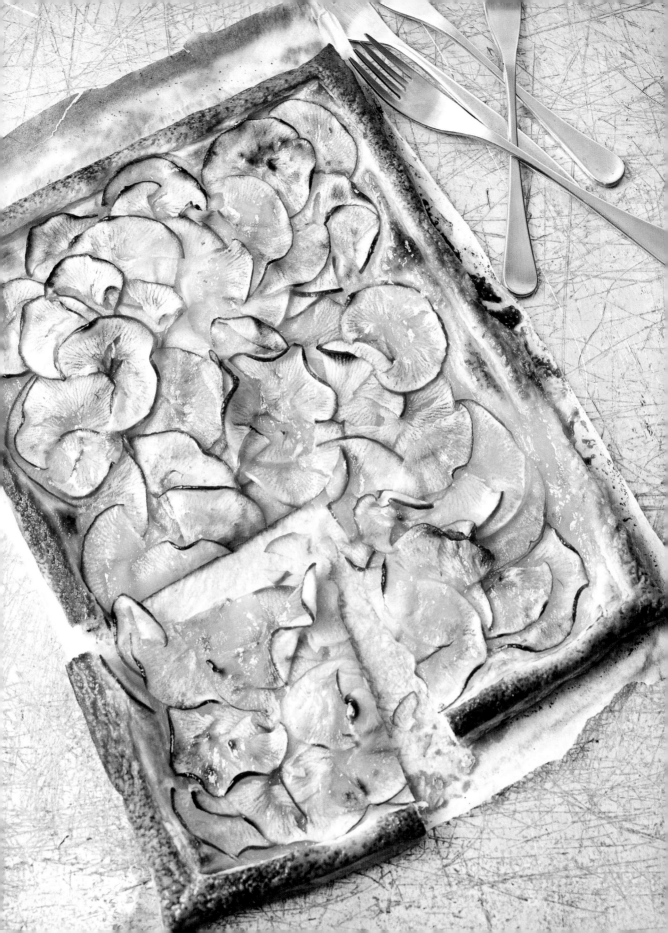

This delicious marmalade is perfect for spreading on toast. It will keep for up to 2 years.

butternut squash and orange marmalade

If using pumpkin, cut it into large chunks. Using a spiralizer fitted with a 3 mm (⅛ inch) spaghetti blade, spiralize the squash or pumpkin. You should end up with about 800 g (1 lb 10 oz) spiralized squash or pumpkin.

Place the spiralized squash or pumpkin in a preserving pan or wide saucepan, add the oranges, lemon juice and ginger, if using, and pour over the measurement water. Bring to the boil, then reduce the heat and simmer for 20–25 minutes or until the oranges are tender.

Add the sugar and cook over a low heat, stirring until it has dissolved. Increase the heat to high and bring to the boil, then reduce the heat to medium and simmer for 25–30 minutes or until the mixture is thick and syrupy and leaves a clear channel when a wooden spoon is drawn through it.

Leave the marmalade to cool in the pan for 5 minutes, then carefully ladle into hot sterilized jars and seal.

Makes about 4 x 250–275 ml (8–9 fl oz) jars

Prepare in 15 minutes

Cook in about 1 hour

1 large or 2 medium butternut squash (the non-bulbous end) or pumpkin, peeled and halved widthways

2 unwaxed oranges, thinly sliced and halved

juice of 2 lemons

75 g (3 oz) fresh root ginger, peeled and thinly sliced (optional)

1 pint (600 ml) water

800 g (1 lb 10 oz) granulated sugar

This instant jam is so quick to make and can be eaten once cooled. Delicious spread on scones or crumpets.

quick apple and ginger jam

Serves 4

Prepare in 5 minutes

Cook in 10–15 minutes

2 Bramley apples, peeled and ends trimmed

4 tablespoons golden caster sugar, or to taste

5 cm (2 inch) piece fresh root ginger, peeled and grated

1 tablespoon lemon juice

Using a spiralizer fitted with a 6 mm (¼ inch) flat noodle blade, spiralize the apples.

Place the spiralized apples in a saucepan with the sugar and ginger. Cook over a medium heat, stirring gently, until the sugar has dissolved. Bring to the boil, then reduce the heat and simmer for 8–10 minutes, until the apple is tender.

Stir in the lemon juice and cook for a further 2–3 minutes, until the jam has thickened and reduced. Leave to cool before serving. The jam will keep for up to 2–3 days in the refrigerator.

This cross between a jam and a marmalade is a great way of using up a glut of courgettes.

courgette, lemon and ginger jam

Using a spiralizer fitted with a 3 mm (⅛ inch) spaghetti blade, spiralize the courgettes. Roughly snip any really long strands in half with scissors.

Place the spiralized courgettes in a preserving pan or wide saucepan with the ginger and lemon rind and juice. Cook over a low heat, stirring occasionally, for 3–4 minutes or until the courgettes start to release their liquid.

Add the sugar and cook gently, stirring until it has dissolved. Increase the heat to high and bring to the boil. Boil for about 15–20 minutes or until the jam has reduced and and is glossy. To test whether the jam is set, place a little on a cold saucer and leave for a few minutes. Gently push the jam with your finger – if it wrinkles it has reached setting point.

Remove from the heat and spoon off any foam from the surface. Leave the jam to cool in the pan for 10 minutes, then carefully pour into hot sterilized jars and seal. The jam will keep for up to 1 year.

Makes about 4 x 450 g (14½ oz) jars

Prepare in 5 minutes

Cook in 20–25 minutes

1 kg (2 lb) courgettes, ends trimmed and halved widthways

75 g (3 oz) piece fresh root ginger, peeled and grated

finely grated rind and juice of 2 unwaxed lemons

1 kg (2 lb) jam sugar

index

acknowledgements

Thank you to dexam.co.uk for loaning us the spiralizers for the photoshoot.

Editorial Director: Eleanor Maxfield
Project Editor: Clare Churly
Copy Editor: Jo Murray
Art Director: Tracy Killick at Tracy Killick Art Direction and Design
Photographer: William Shaw
Home Economist: Denise Smart
Prop Stylist: Liz Hippisley
Production Manager: Caroline Alberti